100
GREATS

AYR UNITED
FOOTBALL CLUB

100 GREATS

AYR UNITED
FOOTBALL CLUB

COMPILED BY
DUNCAN CARMICHAEL

TEMPUS

Frontispiece: Ally MacLeod in contented mood. The public's affinity with him was illustrated by his status as a former Ayr 'Citizen of the Year'.

First published 2004

Tempus Publishing Limited
The Mill, Brimscombe Port,
Stroud, Gloucestershire, GL5 2QG
www.tempus-publishing.com

British Library Cataloguing in Publication Data.
A catalogue record for this book is available from the British Library.

ISBN 0 7524 3089 0

Typesetting and origination by Tempus Publishing Limited
Printed and bound in Great Britain

Acknowledgements

In putting together this project there were no difficulties in submitting the text. It was made easy by the career achievements of the characters contained within these pages. Even allowing for a good personal collection, the illustrations proved to be a different prospect and in this respect I am greatly indebted to Stewart McConnell of the *Ayr Advertiser* and Mike Wilson of the *Ayrshire Post*. I am again glad to record an acknowledgement of the unashamed Ayr United bias displayed by both of these newspapers. Brian Caldwell of Ayr United FC has been similarly helpful in supplying photographs as has Tam Fitzsimmons who is always able to assist in the access of some of the post-war images. Nor has moral support been lacking. Wife Carol, daughter Jill and son David are all Ayr United devotees. David was especially helpful in being able to immediately fix any computer problems and Jill was desperately keen to offer advice on which players should have been included. That advice was not always listened to because some of it was based on players' looks! A negative aspect is that the family had considerably less access to the computer while all this was taking shape. Still, at least it was all in a good cause. A venture aimed at raising the profile of Ayr United heroes just has to be a good cause.

Introduction

Who is the greatest Ayr United great of all? It would not be necessary to canvass public opinion to come up with the answer. With complete certainty it can be stated that Ally MacLeod would be the name offered by all devotees of Ayr United. It is sad to record that he passed away in February 2004 but the memories will never diminish. As a manager he was a natural motivator and his infectious enthusiasm brought out the best in players and fans. It is difficult not to reminisce over glory days when Saturdays were craved over. He truly did represent the spirit of Ayr United.

The '100 Ayr United Greats' contained within these pages do not come to you in order of merit. By presenting the names in alphabetical order, your writer has been absolved of a very heavy responsibility. It was difficult enough just to contain the names to the requisite number since there are more than 100 characters befitting of the status of an 'Ayr United Great'. One hundred is not a large number against the background of a history dating back to 1910 but it is anticipated that the final selection will meet with approval.

The record breakers are all covered. Peter Price, for example, has scored more Ayr United goals than anyone and there is Jimmy Smith who scored a quite extraordinary total of 66 League goals in a single season. Consistent with the goalscoring theme is Alex Ingram who has scored the most Scottish Cup goals for the club. For longevity John Murphy cannot be beaten. He holds the record for the longest career span at the club and, of course, this is consistent with the fact that he remains unsurpassed in the matter of having made the most appearances.

Whenever long-standing fans reminisce it is inevitable that the conversation will turn to the players who were 'crowd pleasers'. Those who have fallen into that category have been endowed with the extra degree of ability required to entertain people in addition to playing effectively. This book will fulfil a very useful purpose by keeping alive the eccentricities of players like

Hyam Dimmer, a footballing maestro who was possessed of a skill which could make beleaguered opponents look very foolish. In their respective eras Cutty Young, John Doyle and Henry Templeton all had the type of close ball control which kept Somerset Park crowds enthralled. The eccentric brilliance of goalkeeper Hugh Sproat also brought much pleasure to the terraces.

Moreover the selection contained herein has taken cognisance of the fact that not every fan prefers the more subtle aspects of football. It is just as befitting to recognise that players categorised as 'hard men' have found their way into local footballing legend. 'Sanny' McAnespie was particularly uncompromising in the face of any attacking threat and the same can be said of Stan Quinn who did not even hold back in training matches. Malcolm Shotton was another who could be similarly categorised. He played football with a smile on his face, even when putting in crunching tackles.

Good times evolve by way of a very simple concept. This is the concept whereby great players bring about great results and, as a logical consequence, the good times roll. Yet every trend is there to be broken and it would be remiss to omit mention of some marvellous players who have appeared in generally struggling Ayr United teams. Eddie Moore was a prime example.

This book bridges a succession of generations right through from the club's formative years; although success is not the exclusive domain of distant history. Conspicuous cup runs in recent years have been instrumental in ensuring a representation of players from the modern age. Ideally there will be consensus over the players selected for inclusion. In reality it is possible that there may be minor areas of disagreement surrounding the issue of players omitted. Yet it would be difficult to dispute that an All-Time Ayr United XI would be drawn from the names you are on the verge of reading about. An All-Time Ayr United XI – now there is a thought! On completing the pages ahead, readers will be suitably qualified to make an informed choice as to the composition of such a team. However that should not divert from the true motive for compiling this book. The purpose of the exercise was to provide a fitting tribute to the best Ayr United players and managers.

100 Club Greats

Garry Agnew
Alec Beattie
Billy Brae
Mark Campbell
Robert Connor
Jacky Cox
Ronnie Coyle
David Craig
Gordon Cramond
Johnny Crosbie
Harry Cunningham
Davy Currie
Gordon Dalziel
Hyam Dimmer
John Doyle
Cammy Duncan
John Duncan
Jacky Ferguson
Jim Fleeting
Rikki Fleming
Derek Frye
Billy Fulton
Willie Furphy
Duncan George
Willie Gibson
Johnny Graham
Ian Hawkshaw
Bob Hepburn
Jimmy Hogg
Gregg Hood
Alain Horace
John Hughes
Glynn Hurst
Alex Ingram

Willie Japp
Johnny Kilgannon
Sam Leckie
Paul Lovering
Ally MacLeod
Dick Malone
Ian McAllister
Alex McAnespie
Neil McBain
Andy McCall
Walker McCall
Phil McCloy
Davy McCulloch
Jim McGhee
Terry McGibbons
Alan McInally
Alastair McIntyre
Willie McIntyre
Switcher McLaughlan
Brian McLaughlin
George McLean
Jim McLean
Jimmy McLeod
Sam McMillan
Norrie McNeil
Willie McStay
Billy Middleton
Dougie Mitchell
Eddie Monan
Eddie Moore
Eric Morris
Malky Morrison
John Murphy
Craig Nelson

Andy Nesbit
Stevie Nicol
George Nisbet
Jim Nisbet
Arthur Paterson
Peter Price
Stan Quinn
Jimmy Richardson
Jacky Robertson
Tommy Robertson
Fally Rodger
Franck Rolling
Bobby Rough
Len Round
Malcolm Shotton
John Sludden
Jimmy Smith
Jock Smith
Peter Smith
Hugh Sproat
Davy Stewart
Gary Teale
Henry Templeton
Frank Thompson
Bobby Thomson
Lewis Thow
Danny Tolland
John Traynor
Andy Walker
Davy Wells
Sprigger White
Cutty Young

The twenty who appear here in italics, occupy two pages instead of the usual one.

Garry Agnew originally played for Ayr Boswell before going to Middlesbrough during season 1988/89. Having been a schoolboy international, his credentials were good but he returned to sign for Kilmarnock. After being released by Kilmarnock at the end of 1990/91, he appeared for Ayr United as a trialist in two pre-season games in a tournament at Fraserburgh. He impressed and terms were agreed. In games against Coventry City and Swansea City, he played well and he became the established left-back.

His competitive debut was in a League fixture at Forfar on 10 August 1991. A late winner secured victory and the early part of the season was marked with a run of victories. Agnew proved to be sound defensively and devastating on the overlap. He was adept at shooting too. Free-kicks in the proximity of the penalty area were a particular strength: 'Mike Smith touched a free-kick to Agnew whose raging left-foot drive flew past Paul Mathers from twenty-five yards' – Ayr United 4 Dundee 1, 29 October 1991. His shooting power was formidable whether he was striking a dead ball or whether the chance was set up: 'Furphy's long ball from midfield was nodded down by Graham at the edge of the box and Garry Agnew equalised with a great left-foot shot' – Kilmarnock 1 Ayr United 1, 1 January 1992. Being a derby goal, that particular strike was appreciated more. 'Agnew carved down the left and cut back a low cross which Walker's neat flick deflected into the path of Bryce whose shot went in via the underside of the bar' – Hamilton Accies 2 Ayr United 1, 11 January 1992. Although the points were conceded on that afternoon, the goal came largely from the persistence of Garry Agnew.

Motherwell won the Scottish Cup in 1991 then began their defence of it in a third-round tie at Ayr in 1992. While pursuing a late equaliser, Agnew cannoned a free-kick against the Motherwell wall with such

velocity that the visiting defenders were left in a state of disarray when the ball broke loose. Duncan George took the opportunity to touch the ball home for a replay. The whole sequence of events typified a common scenario; the crowd anticipated that something special might happen when Garry Agnew ventured upfield. He was named as the Supporters' Association 'Player of The Year' for 1991/92.

Off the field he was a credit to the club, being ever-willing to make public relations visits to local schools. At heart he was also an Ayr United supporter. On a September night in 1992, he was ill before a B&Q Cup tie against St Mirren. He was ordered home but disobeyed by watching the tie from the Somerset Road end. No doubt the last-minute winner prompted a recovery!

On 12 December 1992, he left the field twenty minutes before the end of a 1-0 win at home to Dunfermline Athletic. He was still not twenty-two, yet this was the end of his playing career at senior level. At the time, the severity of his injury was not fully realised and it was assumed that he would eventually return. After two groin operations, he was compelled to concede to the advice of specialists. Not until September 1993 did he quit senior football officially.

During 1993/94, Garry Agnew could be spotted among the fans at home and away matches and, in 1994/95, he ventured a comeback with Cumnock Juniors. During his brief Ayr United career he made a major impression. Alas, it is a sad reflection that the word 'brief' has to be used in this context.

| | League | | Scottish Cup | | League Cup | |
	Apps	Goals	Apps	Goals	Apps	Goals
1991/92	35	4	2	0	3	0
1992/93	18	1	0	0	1	0
	53	5	2	0	4	0

Alec Beattie

Outside left, 1946-1957

At the age of twenty-three, Alec Beattie joined Ayr United from Rangers in August 1946. His debut came in the same month and it was the occasion of six goals being shared with Dundee United at Somerset Park. From mid-September, he began to pick up a scoring consistency which was to make him the club's top scorer for that season.

Beattie's strength was an ability to make mazy runs then put in a dangerous shot or cross. On 1 November 1947, in the course of a 6-2 home win over Dunfermline Athletic, he scored 'four wonderful goals', the last of which came directly from a corner kick. On 6 March 1948, St Johnstone fell 2-1 at Ayr and again he scored directly from a corner kick. Also at Somerset Park, and also in a 2-1 win, he did likewise in a League Cup tie against Dumbarton on 9 October 1948. The feat was further repeated in a 1-1 draw at home to Airdrie on 29 January 1949.

In addition to being adept at scoring from the corner arc, he got other goals from tight angles. On 11 February 1950 he failed to score in a 5-0 home win over Forfar Athletic, but one of his famous corner kicks bounced off the crossbar in what was undoubtedly a deliberate scoring attempt. He was further adept at crashing shots which were routinely described as 'unsaveable'. Just as routine were the goal descriptions which were suffixed by the phrase 'from a Beattie cross'.

In September 1952 a 1-0 win at Kilmarnock produced a personal performance described as 'mesmeric'. One week later he scored twice in a 5-0 deluge of Dumbarton at Ayr. His second goal came in the final minute and he was indulging in his old trick again. It was directly from a corner kick!

Mike McKenna became the favoured choice at outside left and, at the season's end,

Alec Beattie's name was on the list of freed players. He declined terms from Albion Rovers and announced that he had decided to quit football. In June 1953 Reuben Bennett was named as the new Ayr United manager in succession to Archie Anderson. Whether coincidentally, or not, the decision to free Beattie was rescinded. He was destined to be an Ayr United player for the rest of his life.

'Alec Beattie was the best forward on the field' – Ayr United 3 Arbroath 0, 26 December 1953; 'Alec Beattie provided a hot tonic for suffering supporters' – Ayr United 0 Dumbarton 0, 16 January 1954. Such remarks were attributed to a player who had re-signed on a temporary basis. Nevertheless Mike McKenna was the outside left in favour when 1954/55 got underway. Beattie's recall did not take place until December and he proceeded to average a goal per game in his first five games back. Yet these games were at outside right, the position normally occupied by Willie Japp. 'Beattie's corner was returned to him and he netted with a low drive from an acute angle' – Hamilton Accies 5 Ayr United 1, 1 January 1955. Beattie's hallmark was still being stamped!

Alec Beattie's testimonial match had been scheduled for 16 September 1953 with Rangers as the planned visitors. Rangers did play at Ayr on that evening and they lost 3-2. By an unfortunate coincidence they were scheduled to play at Ayr in the second leg of a League Cup quarter-final on that date. The Alec Beattie testimonial match therefore took place on the evening of 21 September 1955. It was organised by the Supporters' Association who ambitiously tried to get Stanley Matthews to play for Ayr United. Rangers were beaten 3-0.

'Alec Beattie's three goals were models of accurate marksmanship' – Ayr United 5 Dumbarton 1, 12 November 1955. This was a promotion-winning season. 'The seemingly ageless veteran, Alec Beattie, jauntily picked his way through the ice patches with a gifted assurance and with cunning body swerves repeatedly left Willie Kilmarnock grovelling in the snow' – Airdrie 3 Ayr United 2 –

abandoned at half-time, 23 February 1957; 'Beattie hooked a glorious goal over his shoulder' – Partick Thistle 5 Ayr United 1, 27 April, 1957. The game just referred to was the concluding fixture of the season and it also brought forth the following comment from the same journalist: 'What would Ayr do without the effervescent Beattie?'. The question was almost prophetic.

On 7 July 1957, he was involved in a motoring accident near his home in the east end of Glasgow. He lay in a coma until passing away on 30 July.

His daughter later married Peter McCloy, who became famous as a Rangers goalkeeper. Their son, Stephen McCloy, was a striker in the Ayr United team which lost to Hibs in the final of the BP Youth Cup in 1992.

	League		Scottish Cup		League Cup	
	Apps	Goals	Apps	Goals	Apps	Goals
1946/47	22	11	2	0	4	2
1947/48	29	11	1	0	5	3
1948/49	29	6	2	0	6	2
1949/50	29	10	1	0	6	2
1950/51	24	6	4	0	9	1
1951/52	14	1	0	0	6	2
1952/53	9	3	0	0	0	0
1953/54	17	5	1	0	0	0
1954/55	19	11	2	2	0	0
1955/56	36	19	2	0	3	2
1956/57	18	4	0	0	1	0
	246	87	15	2	40	14

Stephen McCloy, grandson of Alec Beattie, is pictured here fourth from left in the front row.

Billy Brae
Inside left, 1923-1935

On Saturday 4 August 1923, the new Ayr United manager, Jimmy Richardson, travelled to Glasgow to sign Billy Brae, a twenty-year-old inside forward with Petershill. In his initial season he had to play Alliance League football, although there was a solitary First Division appearance during 1923/24. Regular outside left Jamie McLean broke his leg in a scoreless draw at home to Hamilton Accies and there was a reshuffle for the next match against Clyde at Shawfield on 8 December 1923. Compounding the scene was a 1-0 defeat. The next season saw him have 10 League starts but from 1925/26 he became a regular, albeit in the Second Division. It was the first of five consecutive seasons in which he was the club's second-top League scorer.

Billy Brae had an exceptional 1927/28. He assisted Jimmy Smith towards his record-breaking total of 66 League goals while getting 21 of his own. On the evening of 29 August 1928, he was recognised with a testimonial match which resulted in a 4-1 win over Kilmarnock. This was a successful phase of his career. In a 4-2 home victory over Queen's Park on 20 October 1928, he scored a goal, described thus: 'Brae got possession well out and beat man after man. He finally cut in towards goal, challenged all the way, to wind up with an oblique shot that flashed into the far corner of the net. It was one of the best goals ever scored at Somerset Park.'

Among his goals were less conventional strikes. One came in a visit from Rangers on 18 February 1931. At half-time Ayr United were 2-0 down but Pearson Ferguson pulled one back at the start of the second half. With half an hour left, Billy Brae made it 2-2 after playing a one-two off the referee. That goal finished the scoring.

At the outset of 1932/33 he was a signing rebel and missed the first three League games. Two days before a home match with Aberdeen he relented and played in a 3-1 win.

Two years later he was again in dispute with the club over his contract. Two League games were missed pending resolution. The conclusion of 1934/35 saw relegation coincide with Billy's release. His twelve-year Ayr United career span comprised a club record at the time and he remains one of five players to have surpassed 100 League goals for the club.

In July 1935 he had a trial for Lille but suffered from a rule restricting French clubs to fielding three foreigners. He then joined Swindon Town. He settled in Cheltenham and, in August 1961, returned to Somerset Park to attend Ayr United v. Dumbarton.

| | League | | Ayr Charity Cup | | Scottish Cup | |
	Apps	Goals	Apps	Goals	Apps	Goals
1923/24	1	0	1	0	0	0
1924/25	10	1	1	0	2	0
1925/26	29	12	1	0	1	0
1926/27	36	16	1	0	2	0
1927/28	32	21	1	0	2	0
1928/29	37	11	–	–	2	1
1929/30	38	13	1	0	2	1
1930/31	21	5	–	–	3	1
1931/32	30	8	2	1	2	0
1932/33	33	3	–	–	3	0
1933/34	34	11	2	0	2	0
1934/35	26	3	–	–	3	0
	327	104	10	1	24	3

Mark Campbell
Central defender, 1999-2004

In January 1997, Mark Campbell moved from Maybole Juniors to Stranraer. In February 1999, Ayr United purchased him from Stranraer for £90,000. He was twenty-one, and was immediately in the first-team against Hibs on the last Saturday in February.

Mark Campbell arrived at Ayr when a challenge was being mounted in the First Division and Kilmarnock had recently fallen in a Scottish Cup tie at Somerset Park. Being cup-tied, Campbell was ineligible to play a Scottish Cup tie against Dundee United. He was reinstated on the resumption of the League, being particularly impressive in a 2-0 win at Airdrie on 3 April 1999.

At the outset of the new season, knee trouble kept him out until a comeback against Raith Rovers at Stark's Park. Barely quarter of an hour into the second half, he had to go off. Within five minutes, three goals were conceded and the game ended in a 5-1 defeat.

Niggling injuries prevented him from playing regularly. In 2000 he took no part in the Scottish Cup wins over Dundee and Motherwell, although he did face Partick Thistle in the quarter-finals. With home advantage it was expected that the Second Division opponents would be disposed of. Nevertheless, the tie posed a threat, mainly emanating from Quintin Jacobs. Mark Campbell snuffed him out in a 2-0 win.

His knee trouble was problematic. After playing in the Swedish tour in the summer of 2000, he was unable to start the League season. His comeback was as a half-time substitute at Livingston in September. Campbell hit form and so did the team. Then he had the misfortune to suffer ankle ligament

trouble in October. This time his return was through substitute listings. On being declared fit to start, there were signs that his form had not deserted him. He marked his return with a headed goal in a Scottish Cup tie at Inverness. A three-man central defence evolved, comprising John Hughes, Mark Campbell and David Craig, and a seemingly dead title challenge was revived. Campbell was majestic. A 6-0 win at home to Falkirk, together with his goal, illustrated the form of player and team.

On the last day of March 2001, top spot in the First Division was won from Livingston, although the SPL bosses had asserted that Ayr United would not be promoted. Yet the title was being vigorously pursued and Mark Campbell remained keen to threaten at set pieces. Second place had to be settled for, but Mark Campbell was not risked in the closing matches, being just one booking away from missing the start of 2001/02. It did not matter. On 28 July 2001, he was stretchered off in a friendly with Wigan Athletic with cruciate ligament trouble. He saw no competitive action in 2001/02. As part of his recovery he rehabilitated at Lilleshall. The process was to some avail. At the start of 2002/03, he was made club captain, and played some of the best football of his career in the season ahead. At the end of 2003/04 he signed for Falkirk.

	League		Scottish Cup		League Cup	
	Apps	Goals	Apps	Goals	Apps	Goals
1998/99	9	0	0	0	–	–
1999/00	19	2	2 + 1	0	1	0
2000/01	16 +8	1	1	1	0	0
2001/02	0	0	0	0	0	0
2002/03	28	2	2	0	1	0
2003/04	25 +1	2	1	0	1	0
	97	7	6	1	3	0
	+9 sub. listings		+1 sub. listing			

Robert Connor
Full-back, midfielder, 1977-1984, 1996-1997

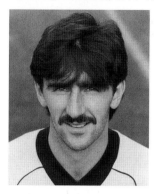

Robert Connor came up from Ayr United Boys Club in summer 1977 and made his first-team debut on 15 March 1978, against Partick Thistle. A 3-1 defeat was suffered but he stayed at left-back.

'The world and his whippet have written off Ayr United as First Division fodder.' These words were penned following his next League match, a 1-0 home loss to St Mirren just days later. The club was heading down, but Connor was the star of that match.

Connor excelled in the First Division. Nicknamed 'Roger', there was one match which allowed that name to be beautifully encapsulated into a headline. The match referred to was a Scottish Cup tie at Dumbarton on 26 January 1980. After winning the game with a penalty kick, a headline read 'ROGER AND OUT'!

Along with teammate Eric Morris, he was in the Scottish League squad to play the League of Ireland at Dublin's Dalymount Park on 17 March 1980. Connor was a substitute,

but international selection at a higher level would eventually come.

In November 1980, Ayr United faced Dundee in the League Cup semi-finals. Reaching a major final for the first time was realistic, as Dundee were a First Division club. Two minutes from the end of the home leg, and trailing 1-0, Connor equalised with a fantastic drive. The away leg was lost 3-2, but that goal remained etched in the memory.

In September 1981, Stevie Nicol and Robert Connor were the Scottish full-backs in an Under-21 international against Sweden. It was a fine honour for a First Division club. By the following year, dissent had crept in among supporters due to poor results. It was no surprise when Connor requested a transfer in October 1982. This was not immediately forthcoming and the club had last-game escapes in 1982/83 and 1983/84. In summer 1984 Connor joined Dundee.

In April 1996 he won his first full cap against Holland. He made three more Scotland appearances while with Aberdeen. On leaving Aberdeen he joined Kilmarnock and completed the circle when he returned to Ayr United in 1996. On 13 August 1996, he scored the goal when Ayr United beat Kilmarnock in the Coca-Cola Cup. The one season of his return was in the Second Division. After winning the Championship, he seemed set for the next season. However, after playing in pre-season, he was released. He joined Partick Thistle, and his next club was Queen of the South. In August 2004 he rejoined Ayr United as a coach.

	League		Scottish Cup		League Cup	
	Apps	Goals	Apps	Goals	Apps	Goals
1977/78	9	0	0	0	0	0
1978/79	27 +3	0	1	0	5	0
1979/80	36 +3	9	2	1	4	0
1980/81	38 +1	8	1	0	10	4
1981/82	28 +2	0	1	1	3 +1	1
1982/83	39	4	1	0	6	0
1983/84	39	7	1	0	2	0
1996/97	18	1	1	0	3	1
	234	29	8	2	33	6
	+9 sub. listings				+1 sub. listing	

Jacky Cox

Jacky Cox was a native of Darvel who broke into senior football with Hamilton Accies. Coincidentally his senior debut was at Somerset Park in the opening League fixture of the 1931/32 season. Matters were tough for any opposing player who clashed with Jacky Cox on his midfield beat. A biography of Rangers legend Bob McPhail contained the following: 'I'll never forget the first time I played against Jacky Cox. I had got the better of him in a dribble somewhere in the middle of the field. As I ran past him he tripped me up, quite deliberately, and sent me flying on my face. I got up and snapped at him "What the hell do you think you are playing at?" With the innocence of a young player he replied, "I was told that if you got the ball past me, then I wasn't to let you past!" What could I say? We became good friends after that little incident and we chuckled over it for years later'.

In 1934/35, Hamilton Accies finished in a creditable fourth place in the First Division table while in the Scottish Cup they lost narrowly to Rangers in the final. This represented the pinnacle of Cox's success with Hamilton and he eventually went to Preston North End.

With war clouds gathering, Ayr United signed two players from Preston in 1939. One of them was striker Terry McGibbons who was rejoining the club. The other was Jacky Cox.

After five matches, the First Division was abandoned in favour of Regional Leagues and a further consequence of war was that full-time contracts had to be scrapped. Jacky Cox was taken on as a shipyard worker. Then, when Ayr United ceased to operate in the summer of 1940, he combined his work with playing for Partick Thistle. He later played for St Mirren and Stranraer. In 1970 Stranraer published a centenary history which stated: 'He was undoubtedly the hardest and most fearless right half ever played by Stranraer.'

Prior to the start of season 1956/57, Ayr United manager Neil McBain agreed to go to Watford for his second spell of management there. The timing meant that the season had to commence without a manager. However a new appointment was made before the completion of the League Cup sectional ties. The new incumbent was Jacky Cox, who had been tempted away from the manager's job at Hamilton Accies.

In 1956/57, the challenge of First Division football proved to be too great but the club returned in 1959 as Second Division champions. Several club records, which still stand, were created during that Championship quest. They were: twenty-eight League wins, seven consecutive away League wins and seventeen consecutive League games unbeaten.

Jacky Cox should have been the first Ayr United manager to take the club into Europe on a competitive basis. There was a tournament called the Anglo-Franco-Scottish Friendship Cup and the participants comprised eight clubs from France, four from England and four from Scotland. Based on the League positions at the conclusion of 1959/60, Ayr United should have qualified for that competition in the season ahead. However that place had to be conceded to Celtic, despite them finishing a place lower. This was due to Somerset Park not being equipped with floodlights. Celtic's first match in the tournament was against Sedan.

In 1960/61 Hearts, the reigning League champions, lost 1-0 at Somerset Park as did Rangers, who were on course for the Championship. Yet these famous victories could not prevent relegation. Jacky Cox resigned on 28 November 1961 and by season 1962/63 he was managing St Mirren. In October 1965 he was spotted at an Ayr United v. Raith Rovers match. At that time he was Fulham's chief scout for Scotland. He died in 1990.

	League	
	Apps	Goals
1939/40	35	0
	First Division (5),	
	Wartime Regional League (30).	

Ronnie Coyle

Central defender, 1996-1997

When Ronnie Coyle arrived at Ayr United, the club had the aim of getting out of the Second Division. He came too late in the 1995/96 season for it to be a realistic ambition in the immediate term but some of the focus was by then being shifted onto the campaign which lay ahead. A year earlier, Simon Stainrod had attempted to negotiate a deal with Raith Rovers. If it had been successful, Franck Rolling would have gone to Raith Rovers in return for Gordon Dalziel and Ronnie Coyle plus £100,000. The offer was turned down due to uncertainty about the future of Raith striker Stevie Crawford. When Coyle signed for the club in March 1996, Gordon Dalziel was his new manager while a transfer fee had already been received for Rolling (from Leicester City). It was ironic that the players and money should have come Ayr United's way after Stainrod had gone.

As a youngster, Ronnie Coyle's potential was proven when Celtic called him up from Celtic Boys Club. On departing Celtic, he joined Middlesbrough and thereafter moved on to Rochdale. The opportunity to return to Scotland was accepted when he put pen to paper for Raith Rovers in 1988.

In stepping into the Second Division with Ayr United, Coyle was able to reflect on having played for Raith Rovers in the UEFA Cup earlier in the same season. That was the background to the situation in which he found himself in opposition to no less a player than Jurgen Klinsmann, then of Bayern Munich. In something of a contrast, he made his Ayr United debut at home to Stirling Albion on 23 March 1996. The result was 2-2 and it formed part of a run in which only one League defeat was inflicted over the course of the season's final sixteen fixtures. Coyle formed a central defensive partnership with John Sharples on that debut. Within the week, the latter was sold to York City.

It was expected that the momentum at the finish to 1995/96 would roll over into 1996/97. The confidence was justified and the assault on the Second Division Championship was under the captaincy of Coyle. A good captain leads by example and that is what he did. Fellow defenders Willie Jamieson and Gregg Hood were more apt to attack at set pieces. Coyle's style was to present himself as a solid defender.

On the last day of the League season, the Second Division Championship trophy was presented to Coyle at Berwick. Yet it could not have been guessed that he had just played his last game for the club. That summer a contract offer was declined on the grounds that it was only for six months. He opted to join Albion Rovers. Subsequent moves took him to East Fife and Queen's Park.

Gordon Dalziel utilised his connections well when he made a sudden transformation to being a manager. Over a period of several years he brought players and coaches to the club, who shared a Raith Rovers connection. Dalziel's move to bring Ronnie Coyle to Ayr United took place during his first season in charge. At that time he was just the type of player the club needed in the quest to escape from the Second Division; an experienced professional who was a good stopper and a good organiser. Ronnie Coyle was captain at a time when only one League defeat was suffered out of the final nineteen League fixtures of the season. Even that one defeat, at Livingston, was a gross injustice.

	League		Scottish Cup		League Cup	
	Apps	Goals	Apps	Goals	Apps	Goals
1995/96	4	0	–	–	–	–
1996/97	29 +1	0	0	0	3	0
	33 +1 sub. listing	0	0	0	3	0

David Craig
Central defender, 1998-2004

David Craig signed for Ayr United in June 1998. Then aged twenty-nine, his former club was Hamilton Accies, having gone there from Raith Rovers. Confusingly, he had originally gone to Raith Rovers from Hamilton Accies! East Stirling and Dundee United were also former clubs of his. His first senior club was Partick Thistle and he had scored his first senior goal for them against Ayr United! It came on 2 December 1989, when the final score was Partick Thistle 1 Ayr United 2.

A hand injury in the opening match of the Swedish tour ruled him out of the start of the season. His debut came in a victorious League Cup tie away to St Mirren on 8 August 1998. 'David Craig was a tower of strength in defence' – Motherwell 0 Ayr United 2, 18 August 1998. In negotiating the next round of the League Cup, this was indicative of his ability. His form was to prove consistently good.

In the air he could outplay the best strikers in the First Division. On the ground he was just as effective. Exponents of the long ball are often criticised but David Craig was skilled at striking them so they found their target.

During the 1999 close season, he sustained a groin injury. He missed the start of the season and unluckily took a bad knock at Falkirk in his second match back. A week later, he was stretchered off with an ankle injury in a home match with Livingston. In the next match, five goals were conceded at Raith Rovers in his absence. In explaining an indifferent start to 1999/00, Gordon Dalziel said: 'I still haven't been able to play David Craig and Mark Campbell together.'

One particularly memorable goal came on the evening of 6 March 2001. A 1-0 lead was held over Falkirk until midway through the second half, when he unleashed a long-range free-kick into the net. It was the first of five goals in fifteen minutes and Ayr won 6-0.

The date 6 February 2002 saw the club reach a national cup final for the first time. Eleven minutes into extra time Eddie Annand scored with a penalty and it was necessary to endure nineteen nerve-wracking minutes to see whether that goal would be enough to win the CIS Cup semi-final. Experienced defending was needed and that is what was supplied. Man of the Match was David Craig.

The point has been made about his sporadic scoring. He gave lie to this on 16 November 2002 when scoring both goals in a win over St Johnstone.

A nickname of 'Big Shyness' gives the wrong impression. David Craig has never been shy about entering fifty-fifty challenges. In September 2004 he was transferred to Queen of the South.

	League		Scottish Cup		League Cup	
	Apps	Goals	Apps	Goals	Apps	Goals
1998/99	22 +1	2	4	0	3	0
1999/00	23	3	4 +1	0	2	0
2000/01	30	1	0 +1	0	0	0
2001/02	27 +1	0	5	0	3	0
2002/03	29 +2	2	2	0	1	0
2003/04	32	1	1	1	1	0
2004/05	1	0	–	–	0	0
	164	9	16	1	10	0
	+4 sub. listings		+2 sub. listings			

Gordon Cramond
Midfielder, 1976-1979

Gordon Cramond was purchased from St Johnstone in March 1976 when Ayr United sat perilously in the Premier League's relegation area. Ayr manager Alex Stuart knew about Cramond's style, having been his boss at Montrose. He then debuted on the ground of the club which he had just left. Crucially the match was won 2-1, and in April 1995 the St Johnstone goalkeeper of 1976, told the *News of the World* that he had thrown the match for a bribe. His story was dismissed.

Prior to Cramond's arrival, Ayr United's last result had been a 5-0 defeat to Dundee United. In something of a transformation, the win at St Johnstone was followed by a home win over Hibs and a crunch away win over Dundee. The influence of Gordon Cramond was apparent and so it continued in a run-in which included a 2-1 win at Celtic Park. Injury prevented him from appearing in the last-game escape in which Motherwell were beaten amid emotional scenes.

Injury further prevented him from starting the 1976/77 season and an observation was made that: 'A fit Gordon Cramond will make a difference in midfield'. That this was true is evidenced by the fact that he was to be named as the Supporters' Association 'Player of The Year'. Once more, however, it was a season in which relegation was a threat. The Scottish Cup was a diversion and a fourth-round tie took Ayr United to Celtic Park on 27 February 1977. Ayr United trailed to a goal which had the defence protesting for offside. With two minutes left, Cramond made it 1-1 after combining with Danny Masterton. Alas, the replay was lost.

On the evening of 6 April 1977, Ayr United played Hearts at Tynecastle Park in what was an ultimate four-pointer. It was a night for strong nerves and, although not tall, Gordon Cramond headed Ayr United in front. In the eighteenth minute, he had to be replaced after pulling a muscle. The result was Hearts 1 Ayr United 2 and it was followed by Ayr United 3 Motherwell 2 on the Saturday. The Motherwell victory came from a Cramond hat-trick.

Ayr United did descend into the First Division in 1978, but Gordon Cramond scored what remains, in the year of writing, the club's last Premier Division goal. It was scored in a 2-0 win at Clydebank in the final match. That summer, Billy McColl was acquired from Clydebank and a set piece was developed. It involved Billy McColl lobbing free-kicks over a defensive wall for Gordon Cramond to meet on the drop and score with a volley. Timing was all important in order to avoid being offside. It was a simple concept which was spectacular to watch.

On Hogmanay 1979 he was sold to Kilmarnock. Tragically, he passed on in 1989 aged thirty-nine

| | League | | Scottish Cup | | League Cup | |
	Apps	Goals	Apps	Goals	Apps	Goals
1975/76	9	0	—	—	—	—
1976/77	23 +5	5	3	1	3	0
1977/78	33 +1	4	0	0	4	3
1978/79	39	5	2	0	6	2
1979/80	18 +2	1	—	—	3	0
	122	15	5	1	16	5
	+8 sub. listings					

Johnny Crosbie

Johnny Crosbie was a native of the Ayrshire mining village of Glenbuck, that famous nursery for great footballers. He played for the quaintly named Glenbuck Cherrypickers before switching allegiance to Muirkirk Athletic and, while there, he came to the attention of Ayr United. Still a teenager, he played two trials for Ayr United reserves. Terms were offered and accepted. He signed for the club on Monday 6 October 1913.

Crosbie made his first-team debut at the age of seventeen. The occasion was a friendly at Somerset Park on New Year's Day 1914 when Ayr United defeated Northern Nomads (an English-Irish combination) 6-4. Two days later he made his League debut in a 2-1 defeat against Hearts at Tynecastle Park.

After the outbreak of war in August 1914, Johnny Crosbie was the first Ayr United player to join up. December 1914 brought a fixture at Dundee while he was conveniently stationed at Cupar with the Lanarkshire Yeomanry. He was permitted to play at Dens Park and he assisted in a 3-2 win.

His appearances were seriously curtailed while serving King and country but his presence was influential when his services could be called upon. For example in September 1916 the team won 2-1 at Kilmarnock and it was reported that: 'Forward one man outshone all others – Johnny Crosbie'.

In December 1916 he was joined in the Ayr United team by another inhabitant of Glenbuck. That player was Alex Shankly of Glenbuck Cherrypickers, an outside left. He was the much-older brother of the better remembered Bill Shankly.

In April 1919, Ireland and Scotland contested a 0-0 draw at Windsor Park, Belfast. Johnny Crosbie played at inside right while his Ayr United teammate Jimmy Richardson played at centre forward. Being a Victory International this was deemed to be unofficial but full international recognition was forthcoming. While still an Ayr United player he appeared for Scotland in a 1-1 draw against Wales at Cardiff in February 1920 and, while with Birmingham City, he played in Scotland's 1-0 win over England at Villa Park in April 1922. At a future date one of his

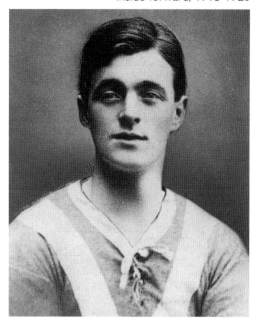

cousins, Jim Nisbet, also a native of Glenbuck, would also represent Scotland while still attached to Ayr United.

In September 1919 he was joined in the Ayr United team by another cousin, Billy Crosbie. In a 5-0 rout of Kilmarnock both Crosbies scored and this was two days before Billy's transfer transaction was written into the club's account books. The conclusion could be conveniently drawn that he was quickly repaying a slice of the transfer fee. It would not have been difficult. Ayr United paid Vale of Clyde the modest sum of seven pounds for him.

On the Wednesday afternoon of 5 May 1920, Johnny Crosbie signed for Birmingham City and the transfer fee was in stark contrast to that of cousin Billy. Initial speculation put the figure at 'about £3,000'. This was based on the fact that Newcastle United's £3,000 offer had been outbid. The speculation was reasonably accurate. Ayr United received £2,800 plus a further sum of £54 5s 3d in interest due to payment not being made until the following March. This money was most useful. In January 1920 the club agreed to buy Somerset Park from landlord W.G. Walker's. The arrangement was to pay five annual instalments of £500. The first payment was made in June 1920 but, for no doubt valid reasons, the payment amounted to £536 10s 4d. Yet the sale of Johnny Crosbie accrued more than was required to purchase Somerset Park outright.

The move to Birmingham City brought quick success when the club won the Second Division Championship in 1920/21. In 1931 he was in their FA Cup final team. The end of the next season saw him released by Birmingham City after a twelve-year playing association with the club. He was held in such regard that he was granted a testimonial twice. In the summer of 1932 he joined Chesterfield and it is also on record that he later played for Blackpool.

When Ayr United resumed football after the Second World War, speculation linked him to the managerial vacancy. It was nothing more than speculation. In reality he did not even apply for the post, instead preferring to remain resident in Birmingham.

However he did come back to spend his last days in Ayr, staying locally at Blackfriars. During this time he made a return to Somerset Park in September 1979 but his visit was not on a match day. He walked out onto the ground where his senior career had begun as a seventeen-year-old. He was now aged eighty-three.

In February 1982 Johnny Crosbie passed away.

	League		Ayr Charity Cup		Victory Cup		Scottish Cup	
	Apps	Goals	Apps	Goals	Apps	Goals	Apps	Goals
1913/14	8	0	1	0	—	—	—	—
1914/15	5	3	—	—	—	—	—	—
1915/16	16	4	1	0	—	—	—	—
1916/17	36	6	—	—	—	—	—	—
1917/18	31	8	—	—	—	—	—	—
1918/19	22	7	1	1	1	0	—	—
1919/20	40	16	—	—	—	—	3	0
	158	44	3	1	1	0	3	0

It may seem that the designation 'forward' is a little vague but it is illustrative of the diversity of positions occupied by Harry 'Peerie' Cunningham. After signing from Cumnock Juniors he was even played as a full-back for Ayr United reserves before the 1920/21 season. At that stage a journalist wrote: 'We cannot understand why a player of Cunningham's stamp is not figuring in Scottish League football... In any position in any team he is an outstanding player.'

His first-team debut came in a First Division fixture at Airdrie on the Wednesday afternoon of 9 February 1921. Cunningham made the team in place of Donald Slade, a thirty-two-year-old whose career had included Southampton (his local club), Lincoln City, Woolwich Arsenal, Fulham and Dundee. In contrast Cunningham's experience had been gained in Ayrshire junior football and in the Alliance League with Ayr United reserves. Glowing reports of his form in reserve matches could not be ignored and his debut brought a win (2-1 to Ayr) but no goals.

In December 1921 it was reported that George Nisbet and Harry Cunningham were the only ever-present players to that point of the 1921/22 season. Cunningham was soon stricken by a nasty injury picked up during a visit from Rangers on 7 January 1922. He had broken a bone in his left leg. His season was over and he only reappeared in 1922/23.

On the last day of September 1922, Third Lanark won 2-1 at Somerset Park. Harry Cunningham had played at centre forward in a 4-0 demise at Motherwell a week earlier but was not listed for the Third Lanark match. The *Ayrshire Post*'s football journalist, John Calderwood, had this to say about his replacement: 'The management seem to have lost all powers of judgement. The directors cannot have studied the physical build and abilities of that young man or they would never have thought of him as a centre forward'. This was in an age when the directors picked the team then gave out the details to the press so that the fans knew what the team would be the day before the match. The *Post*'s Calderwood was a hard-liner and he would occasionally refer back to football in Ayr in the 1880s. He had no fear of offending anyone and presumably his written attack was justified. Whether through external pressure or otherwise, the centre forward one week later was John Quinn and his inside men were Harry Cunningham and Murdoch McKenzie.

The nickname 'Peerie' implies that he could turn quickly while also being able to score slick goals. He also packed a good shot. On 9 February 1924, before a 16,721 Somerset Park crowd, he scored with a twenty-yard drive to eliminate Kilmarnock from the Scottish Cup. This tie was filmed by Green's Cinema. If only the footage had survived!

Although individually talented, Ayr United were relegated in 1925 and Cunningham joined Kilmarnock, where he got a Scottish Cup winners' medal in 1929. John Thomson, the legendary Celtic 'keeper, claimed the best save he ever made was from Harry Cunningham in a Kilmarnock match.

'Peerie' was well-known locally and lived in Ayr's Kyle Street until his death in 1972.

| | League | | Ayr Charity Cup | | Scottish Cup | |
	Apps	Goals	Apps	Goals	Apps	Goals
1920/21	13	3	1	0	2	0
1921/22	27	7	0	0	0	0
1922/23	29	7	0	0	3	1
1923/24	37	9	1	0	7	4
1924/25	35	7	0	0	2	1
	141	33	2	0	14	6

Davy Currie

Centre half, 1933-1940

Davy Currie was relatively old when joining Ayr United from junior football. Born on 3 March 1907, he came from Cambuslang Rangers for his debut on 18 February 1933 in a 1-1 draw with Morton.

In junior football he had excelled and been an international at that level. It is therefore difficult to grasp why he did not play senior football sooner. During his time at Ayr he opposed some highly rated centre forwards, one of whom was the famous Jimmy McGrory who amassed 410 League goals in a fabulous career. In response to a 3-1 win over Celtic at Somerset Park on 18 November 1933, the following was written: 'Imagine McGrory (metaphorically) bound hand and foot – and gagged into the bargain! Currie did that single-handed.' The return League engagement took place on 24 March 1934 and, Ayr United's margin of victory was 3-0. It was considered that the match had given the Scotland selectors cause for concern. Kennaway, McGonagle and McGrory had been candidates for the looming Wembley international but neither managed to show up well in the Ayr match. McGrory had been well held by Davy Currie. Again!

On 30 March 1935, Dundee were defeated 3-2 at Ayr in a gruesome spectacle. An *Ayrshire Post* headline exclaimed: 'Ayr Win Roughest Game In Years'. Inevitably the fixture was not victim-free. The victim was Davy Currie who sustained such a severe injury that he did not make a further League appearance until late November. Willie Clark, signed from Larkhall Thistle, deputised. When Currie returned, the club's First Division status was looking fragile. His comeback was made in the third of six consecutive League defeats. Ultimately relegation could not be halted. More positively it can be stated that only one of his peacetime seasons with Ayr was in that lower sphere. Yet there was almost a return to the Second Division in 1938 when a scoreless draw at home to Dundee saved Ayr United from relegation on the final day. Defeat would have put the club down while the visitors had to win to stay up. It was a day for steady nerves in defence, and a journalist penned that: 'Currie was the bulwark of the home team'.

Talk emerged of a testimonial. Unfortunately it was spoken of during the 1939 close season. The war cost him a testimonial and his career. His last match for the club was a wartime Regional League fixture against Queen's Park on 10 February 1940, a 2-1 defeat.

He died aged eighty-six on 10 February 1994. It signified the passing away of a former Ayr United captain for whom the description 'bulwark' summarised his play.

| | League | | Ayr Charity Cup | | Scottish Cup | |
	Apps	Goals	Apps	Goals	Apps	Goals
1932/33	9	0	—	—	—	—
1933/34	37	1	2	0	2	0
1934/35	35	0	—	—	5	0
1935/36	19	1	2	0	1	0
1936/37	33	0	—	—	1	0
1937/38	38	1	2	0	7	0
1938/39	38	1	—	—	1	0
1939/40	8	0	—	—	—	—
	217	4	6	0	17	0

The void League match versus Falkirk on 9 March 1935 has been included as an appearance.
1939-40: First Division (2), Wartime Regional League (6).

Gordon Dalziel

Striker, 1995-1996; manager, 1995-2002

When Gordon Dalziel signed for Ayr United on 7 July 1995, it was considered to be a major coup. He came as a striker of considerable repute, having played for Rangers, Manchester City, Partick Thistle, East Stirling and Raith Rovers. In the season recently finished, Raith Rovers had qualified for the UEFA Cup by winning the Coca-Cola Cup. Dalziel therefore left the club on a high and he remains their highest goalscorer of all time.

He came to Ayr principally as a striker, but also as a coach. Ayr United had finished the 1994/95 season with Justin Jackson as the club's top scorer in the League. How many goals did he net in order to achieve top-scorer status? Four, to be precise! It was hoped that Dalziel would be a saviour to the club by dint of scoring a large number of goals. He was to succeed in making a major contribution to the fortunes of the club, but it was not anticipated that this contribution would be in management. In the year of writing, he remains the club's second-longest serving manager of all time; second only to Ally MacLeod.

On 2 September 1995, Berwick Rangers won 4-1 in a Second Division fixture at Somerset Park. In concise terms, the best definition was 'debacle'. Simon Stainrod quit on the Monday and Gordon Dalziel was installed as interim manager. His first test in management comprised a visit from Forfar Athletic and he admitted to experiencing pre-match nerves. Although he scored in the match, it was lost 3-1. Injury prevented him from reappearing for the second half and his irritation was doubtlessly compounded by realising the magnitude of the managerial task ahead. On 31 October 1995, it was announced that the job belonged to Dalziel on a permanent, rather than an interim basis. It was further announced that Ally Dawson, a former Rangers captain and Scottish international, would be joining the club as his assistant. On the following Saturday, Stirling Albion won 2-1 at Somerset Park. It comprised Ayr United's last home defeat of the season. Dalziel quickly became a workaholic. His desire to nurture a successful Ayr United team became an obsession. This

manifested itself in a large turnover of players as he strove relentlessly to get things right. Safety from relegation in 1995/96 then the Second Division Championship in 1996/97; these were the result of his labours.

In the complex world of transfer manoeuvres, he had the advantage of being excellent at selling prospective new players the benefits of coming to Ayr. This ability to market the club explained why he was able to acquire players who were sought after by rival clubs. The gradual progression manifested itself in good vocal backing, with Dalziel being one of the names which was regularly regaled in song.

In 1995/96, Ayr United used a total of forty-five players in competitive matches. Two seasons later, the number was forty-six. There were supporters who considered such a turnover to be acceptable grounds for criticism. Yet the alternative theory was that these were the actions of a man who was striving hard for success.

At the end of 1998/99, the club occupied third place in the First Division table. It was the loftiest finishing position for an Ayr United team since 1979/80. The completed table of 2000/01 involved finishing second. One year earlier, Dunfermline Athletic had been granted promotion on attaining that position. Third place was again achieved in 2001/02, although the Dalziel years will be remembered not only for high League placings. His high-profile cup successes generated great excitement. In his years of management, it was virtually expected that clubs from a higher League would become victims of Ayr United. In the Scottish Cup, such victims comprised Kilmarnock (twice), Dundee, Motherwell, Dunfermline Athletic and Dundee United. In the League Cup, his successes against clubs from higher Leagues comprised Kilmarnock (twice), Motherwell, and Hibs. In the time span involved, this was astonishing. Ten acts of supposed giant-killing! In reality it became a matter of routine rather than giant-killing. The media regularly posed the question as to how this could be reconciled with an inability to win

the First Division title. There was a simple answer and it was all down to the standard of First Division football being much higher than it was given credit for.

On St Patrick's Day 2002, Gordon Dalziel became the first ever manager to lead an Ayr United team out at a national cup final. These were emotional moments when the team emerged at Hampden to face Rangers in the CIS Cup final. In the club's history, the semi-finals of the Scottish Cup have been reached three times in the year of writing; 1973, 2000 and 2002. Dalziel took the club to all but the first. Only a missed penalty against Dundee United in 1999 prevented it from being three Scottish Cup semi-finals out of four.

On 20 November 2002, he voluntarily stepped down as manager and was succeeded by Campbell Money. He remained at the club as a coach until November 2003. In June 2004 he became manager of Glenafton Athletic and in October of that year he filled the managerial vacancy at Raith Rovers.

	League		Scottish Cup		League Cup	
	Apps	Goals	Apps	Goals	Apps	Goals
1995/96	16	4	1	0	0	0
	+7 sub. listings					

Hyam Dimmer

Inside forward, 1935-1940

On Friday 2 August 1935, a junior match ended Kilsyth Rangers 2 Croy Celtic 2. Interested spectators were Ayr United manager Frank Thompson and director Jimmy Frew. Their attention was on Kilsyth's Hyam Dimmer, from Scotstoun, who had already played in a public trial match at Somerset Park. After the match he agreed to join Ayr United.

His first-team debut was against Rangers on 17 August 1935. It was a 2-2 draw and Dimmer was praised for his cool. Following relegation to the Second Division his career took off. Reports agreed on his style: 'Though keeping a solemn poker face, he had the crowd in a good humour with his football wizardry and cheeky capers' – Ayr United 6 Forfar Athletic 1, 5 September 1936; 'Dimmer surely must be football's number one entertainer but under the comedy is a definite purpose' – Ayr United 8 Montrose 1, Boxing Day 1936. Despite the theory that he preferred to make goals, Dimmer netted 25 himself in the Championship season.

He replicated his tricks in the First Division. Queen's Park were beaten 6-2 on the day the Second Division Championship flag was unfurled. It was noted that: 'Dimmer had defenders running in circles and the crowd laughing.' On 15 January 1938, Morton lost at Ayr 6-2 and there was another opportunity for lyrical prose: 'Dimmer is a born footballer but his dilly-dallying aroused the alternate delight and ire of the spectators.' One of his goals against Morton was thus described: 'The lanky Dimmer stooped to the occasion and headed another goal.' This implied that he would rather have been using his skills ostentatiously. 'Dimmer tried some

of his surrealist stuff on an opposition which did not appreciate art' – St. Mirren 1 Ayr United 2, 19 February 1938; 'Hyam Dimmer's complexity [...] upset him as much as his opponents. More often than not [...] he contrived to extricate himself from his gyroscopic contortions – that his victims were as lucky was not always apparent' – Ayr United 4 Kilmarnock 0, 7 May 1938.

The opening fixture of 1938/39 brought Raith Rovers to Ayr. Analysis of Ayr's 2-1 win referred to the 'imaginative meanderings of Dimmer'. But with war clouds gathering, his fun was ending. Limited availability in the first wartime season was followed by Ayr United ceasing to operate in 1940.

On New Year's Day 1945, he was spectating at a match between the Western Command and the Scottish Command at Somerset Park. He was approached by officials from Newton Rovers for whom he agreed to play. At this time he had a fruit business in Glasgow. By summer 1946 he was working in England and joined Aldershot. He returned to Somerset Park for an Ayr United v. Cowdenbeath tie in the League Cup on 30 August 1961.

In 1990 the author received a letter from his son. It relayed that Hyam Dimmer had died following a fall. The same letter expressed: 'He never made a thing about his time as a professional footballer and whenever it was mentioned he always used to play it down.'

| | League | | Ayr Charity Cup | | Scottish Cup | |
	Apps	Goals	Apps	Goals	Apps	Goals
1935/36	15	1	1	0	0	0
1936/37	34	25	–	–	1	0
1937/38	28	8	2	1	7	4
1938/39	13	2	–	–	–	–
1939/40	5	1	–	–	–	–
	95	37	3	1	8	4

1939/40: First Division (1), Wartime Regional League (4).

John Doyle was signed from Viewpark Boys Guild in May 1970 and, at the outset of the 1970/71 season, he was given an excellent opportunity. Cutty Young's suspension meant that he was pitched straight into the first team. The League Cup sectional ties began with Tommy Reynolds on the right wing and John Doyle on the left wing. After the first two matches, Doyle was switched to the right and his form was so good that it was wondered what Ally MacLeod would do on the termination of Young's suspension. Cutty Young did regain the number seven shirt and Doyle reverted to playing on the left. Both had the capability to run opposition defences ragged. As a consequence both were apt to be on the wrong end of some cynical tackling. At Falkirk on 24 October 1970, Doyle was sent off three minutes from the end. The misdemeanour was throwing a punch at Jim Shirra after the latter had downed him with a hefty challenge.

Young's departure in the summer of 1971 meant that John Doyle could now play in his best position on a regular basis. The shirt worn by a player of supreme quality then became worn by another player of high calibre.

'He (John Doyle) ran from midfield evading tackle after tackle, before finally scoring as Tommy Gemmell made a desperate effort to stop him' – Celtic 4 Ayr United 1, 30 August 1971. It was an individual goal of the utmost brilliance, although it was illustrative that full-backs often made desperate attempts to stop him. 'John Doyle spent most of the afternoon hurdling high tackles' – Ayr United 0 Motherwell 0, 26 February 1972. He was a traditional Scottish winger who bore the brunt of traditional Scottish tackling. Yet that observation should be qualified with an explanation that he only bore the brunt of such tackling when he could be caught. For example: 'John Doyle had the 'legs' of the Rangers defensive left flank' – Ayr United 2 Rangers 1, 2 September 1972. He also scored in that match. 'A great goal which left the Partick defence in tatters' – Ayr United 2 Partick Thistle 1, 7 October 1972. Although normally a provider, rather than a scorer, that goal was a typical Doyle strike. This was the season of the famous 5-1 victory away to Partick Thistle in the Scottish Cup quarter-finals. Doyle was heavily involved in this tie and his performance culminated with a goal in the final minute. In the month prior to that match, he had played for Scotland against England in an Under-23 international at Kilmarnock. At the end of the season he was in Willie Ormond's pool for the Home Internationals.

On 27 October 1973, an Ayr United win at Dundee, together with a Celtic win against Hearts, would have put Ayr United on top of the First Division table that evening. Celtic fulfilled their part but there was a contributory factor in Ayr's 2-1 defeat at Dens Park. With less than a quarter of the match played, John Doyle was suffering the effects of a very bad tackle from Tommy Gemmell. He soldiered on until being replaced at half-time. Gemmell was only booked and Ally MacLeod was understandably raging. Apart from a temporary return on 24 November, John Doyle did not return to the first team until 2 February 1974 when a 1-1 draw was contested with St Johnstone at Perth. After that match he was described as 'Ayr's liveliest forward'.

Season 1974/75 was littered with bookings for John Doyle. The key reason, of course, was his response to harsh tackling. Matters came to a head on 1 March 1975 when he was sent off for a retaliatory kick after being deliberately obstructed by Airdrie's Paul Jonquin. On his way back to the home dressing room, Doyle threw his chewing gum at the linesman in sheer frustration.

'John Doyle was magnificent' – Ayr United 3 Rangers 0, 11 October 1975. It was this type of form which brought him a full international cap. He lined up for Scotland in a 1-1 draw against Romania at Hampden Park on 17 December 1975. On 18 February 1976, in a Scottish Cup replay away to Queen of the South, he played his last game for Ayr United. After serving a suspension he was sold to Celtic during the following month.

While still a Celtic player, John Doyle electrocuted himself in a domestic accident on 19 October 1981. It was a tragic end to a brilliant footballing talent.

	League		Scottish Cup		League Cup	
	Apps	Goals	Apps	Goals	Apps	Goals
1970/71	13 +2	1	1	0	6	0
1971/72	34	3	3	0	6	1
1972/73	34	6	4	1	6	0
1973/74	23	1	2	0	6	0
1974/75	28	7	1	0	5	1
1975/76	23	6	3	1	6	1
	155	24	14	2	35	3
	+2 sub. listings					

Cammy Duncan
Goalkeeper, 1991-1996

Cammy Duncan did not play for Ayr United in a 'golden age'. Neither was he flamboyant. He could display superb agility but he only did so when necessary. He was, quite simply, a very good goalkeeper.

His first senior club was Sunderland. In 1987 he returned to his native Lanarkshire to sign for Motherwell. At a fee of £60,000, he was sold on to Partick Thistle in 1989. In March 1991, aged twenty-five, he moved to Ayr United in a swap deal for midfielder Sammy Johnston. Manager George Burley had played at Motherwell at the same time as Duncan. Johnston was a good player and it said much that Burley rated his new goalkeeper as valuable.

His Ayr debut came in a 2-2 draw at Brechin on 23 March 1991. In the weeks ahead, relegation fears were banished. Then came a new season which had a startling opening. Four straight League wins were recorded at the beginning of 1991/92. In addition there was a Skol Cup run in which Dundee and St Johnstone were eliminated prior to Hibs winning a quarter-final tie at Ayr. During this time, Duncan was in typically splendid form. Then, following a home match with Partick Thistle on the first Saturday of September, he was out through injury. After regaining his place, an even greater misfortune befell him. On 23 November 1991, while playing in a First Division fixture at Meadowbank Thistle, he collided with teammate Nigel Howard. It was diagnosed that he had a ruptured cruciate ligament at the back of the knee. During the next month, a surgeon at Monklands Hospital told him that his footballing days were over. A London surgeon disagreed. He claimed that with proper training and by building up his thighs, a comeback was viable. This came in pre-season friendlies in July 1992.

August 1992 involved a busy schedule of six League fixtures and a Skol Cup tie. In the last of these matches, at Hamilton, Duncan seemed to face an onslaught on his own during a 1-1 draw. His form was inspirational.

Duncan was adept at absorbing pressure. On 9 January 1993, when Dunfermline lead 2-1 in a Scottish Cup tie, the home team piled forward in desperate hope of forcing a replay. By reason of Duncan's form it remained precisely that! There were occasions in 1993 when the team lost despite his heroics. Games were narrowly lost which might have been heavily lost. An injury at Dunfermline in December 1993 meant that he was unable to play until 12 March 1994; his comeback also being against Dunfermline. In time, recurring injury problems would further blight his career.

On relegation to the Second Division in 1995, Duncan escaped criticism and he deserved to. Manager Simon Stainrod would praise his goalkeeper but he was telling people what they already knew. Injury barred Duncan from starting the 1995/96 season. He did make a respectable number of appearances but the decision to free him at the end of that campaign was assuredly influenced by a failure to get rid of his injury woes. He signed for Albion Rovers, his local club.

	League Apps	Scottish Cup Apps	League Cup Apps
1990/91	11	–	–
1991/92	15	0	3
1992/93	41	2	1
1993/94	31	0	1
1994/95	29	1	1
1995/96	21	1	0
	148	4	6

John Duncan
Full-back, 1948-1950

John Duncan, nicknamed 'Dally', was a Glasgow boy who signed for Ayr United in March 1948, aged twenty-one. He had been demobbed two months earlier. During military service he had played in the same battalion team as Ayr United goalkeeper Len Round. Owing to the timing of the transaction, he remained with his club Partick Avondale for what remained of 1947/48.

Manager Bob Ferrier had no qualms about picking John Duncan right from the start of 1948/49. That season began with a 4-2 League win over St Johnstone at Perth. It was considered that Duncan put in 'a sound display'. One week later, two more League points were picked up at Kilmarnock on a sodden pitch. Even in such conditions, Ayr United's play was described as 'high-speed football'. The pace would not have troubled John Duncan, a former army sprint champion.

Duncan had a reputation for shooting but not for goalscoring. For example, on the evening of 15 September 1948, the Somerset Park crowd witnessed him unleash a forty-yard drive. The force of the shot caused the Stenhousemuir goalkeeper to drop it and Jock Wallace easily scored. Future matches were to see other examples of players feeding off the scraps of Duncan's tendency to have-a-go.

On 20 November 1948, Queen's Park played Ayr in the League. During the match, a penalty was awarded which would normally have been taken by Andy Nesbit. Since Nesbit was being rested, the responsibility was given to Duncan, who had never taken a penalty in senior football. Facing him was Ronnie Simpson, who would one day immortalise himself as one of Celtic's Lisbon Lions. Duncan proceeded to net with 'a rocket shot'. The referee ordered a retake. It is on record that he 'netted another rocket shot'.

Queen's Park revisited for a first-round Scottish Cup tie on 22 January 1949. With

the score at 1-1, and three minutes to go, a free-kick was awarded after Tommy Ramsay was brought down just outside the area. Spectators started shouting for Duncan to take it. His free-kick was struck typically hard and the ball beat the defensive wall before thundering off the underside of the crossbar. Ronnie Simpson got a fist to the ball but Jock Aitken pounced for the winner. It was the familiar story of Duncan causing havoc by shooting though not scoring.

On the evening of 10 May 1950, Ayr United lost 2-1 in a friendly against Newcastle United, at Ashington. Future events rendered it almost certain that Duncan impressed in this match, albeit that six months were to elapse before a bid was made. Newcastle manager Stan Seymour watched Duncan in a 1-1 draw at Stirling on 11 November 1950. It was his last match for Ayr United prior to his transfer to Newcastle United.

Towards the end of season 1951/52, he suffered a knee injury when playing for Newcastle. It was sufficiently serious to force him to retire. Naturally there was talk of a benefit match. After years of procrastination there was agreement. Ayr United were to play Newcastle at Somerset Park on 5 August 1961. The Scottish Football Association prevented the match from happening, claiming that it could not be played before the official start of the season. John Duncan's benefit never took place.

| | League | | Scottish Cup | | League Cup | |
	Apps	Goals	Apps	Goals	Apps	Goals
1948/49	30	1	2	0	6	0
1949/50	20	0	1	0	3	0
1950/51	8	0	–	–	9	0
	58	1	3	0	18	0

Jacky Ferguson's early career began with Minishant Amateurs. His next move was to Annbank United. From there he went senior with Morton. In terms of age, Ferguson was unfortunate in having to do national service. He was in the last wave of conscripts prior to the scheme being abandoned. Yet it was not particularly to the detriment of his football career. While serving in the army in Germany, he took part in representative matches. He was also permitted the luxury of flying home on the Friday in order to play for Morton on the Saturday. Offers to play club football in Germany were declined.

Shortly before being demobbed, he was transferred to Clyde. The next transfer was to Airdrie at which time he trained at Somerset Park. His next transfer took him to Southend United. He was released in the summer of 1968, at which time he consented to becoming an Ayr player.

Jacky Ferguson told the author that Ally MacLeod was the type of manager who made his players feel great. It is a point which any Ayr player of that era would endorse. More important to relate is that this approach had the desired effect. In that first season, Ferguson was initially a winger, prior to being selected as an inside forward. At least he was described as an inside forward! Football was going through a transition in which the 2-3-5 line-up was being phased out. It took longer for the old-fashioned football terminology to be similarly consigned to history.

A goal was forthcoming on his competitive debut. That was in a 3-1 win at home to Cowdenbeath in a League Cup sectional tie. One year later, with promotion having been won, the whole profile of the club was raised. The opening First Division fixture of 1969/70 was truly memorable for a 3-0 win at home to a much-vaunted Hibs team. Ferguson's contribution to the match extended to scoring as well.

'Alex Ingram nodded down to the waiting Ferguson who launched himself at the ball to head past the unhappy Neef to make it 2-0' – Ayr United 2 Rangers 1, 13 September 1969. That particular goal marked the occasion of the ground record being broken. The League Cup semi-final (plus replay) with Celtic, took place in the following month. It ensured that these were exciting times for Jacky Ferguson and for everyone connected to Ayr United.

In season 1970/71, he had a good start. For example in September 1970 he twice scored two goals in League fixtures (Morton away and Clyde at home). Nevertheless he was in the eve of his senior career and was released at the end of that season. His wish was to stop playing but he consented to play for Cumnock Juniors. His next job in football was to manage Maybole Juniors and he later went to Annbank United in a similar capacity, although one day returning to assist Maybole again. Jacky Ferguson also coached Craigmark Burntonians and Darvel Juniors. In the year of writing he was a coach with Lugar Boswell.

His brother Bert, a winger, broke into the Ayr United first team in 1973/74 after joining the club from Maybole Juniors.

	League		Scottish Cup		League Cup	
	Apps	Goals	Apps	Goals	Apps	Goals
1968/69	32	8	2	0	8	1
1969/70	26 +1	3	1	0	10	4
1970/71	10 +2	5	0	0	5 +1	1
	68	16	3	0	23	6
	+3 sub. listings				+1 sub. listing	

Jim Fleeting
Central defender, 1979-1983

Jim Fleeting's football career developed in his native Ayrshire. He played amateur football for Knockentiber and junior football for Kilbirnie Ladeside. His career progression took him to Norwich City and, after walking out on that club, he began training at Somerset Park. Fleeting's credentials were impressive. He had played in the North American Soccer League for Tampa Bay Rowdies. Opponents had included Franz Beckenbauer and George Best. He had also played in the North American Soccer League final in front of a 79,000 crowd.

A move to sign him for Ayr United would probably have taken place in November 1978, had it not been for the obstacle of Norwich City requiring a transfer fee. The sensible option was to give him a trial spell but that was hindered by weather conditions. Eventually he was given a run out in a First Division fixture at home to Stirling Albion on 10 February 1979. That match was won 2-0. He retained his place for a 4-0 home win over Queen of the South in a Scottish Cup tie. Norwich City accepted less than half of the £25,000 transfer fee initially requested. It was astute business from Ayr United.

'Jim Fleeting was immaculate. He marshalled the defence well' – Clyde 0 Ayr United 5, 28 February 1979. This result came in the midweek following Montrose's second 5-0 defeat at Somerset Park that season.

On 7 April 1979, Fleeting was captain of the team for the first time. His organisational ability made him a good choice and a 3-2 win was recorded at Arbroath. 'Led superbly by captain Jim Fleeting, Ayr looked every inch Championship contenders' – Stirling Albion 0 Ayr United 2, 9 February 1980. The Ayr team at this time was rich in individual talent and Championship aspirations seemed realistic. However, at the outset of 1980/81, Ayr United remained in the First Division. Yet promotion hopes were again high. The route to the League Cup semi-finals was strewn with Premier League victims and Fleeting continued to exude authority. Manager Willie McLean had a quality squad of players at his disposal and this was borne out by results. But the momentum slowed and the pattern was repeated in 1981/82. Then, in 1982/83, there was no promotion push at all. Jim Fleeting was released at the end of that season, although he had received advance notice of his departure.

He later played for Clyde and managed Kilmarnock. On the field, one of his great strengths had been his organisational ability. It was a strength which he was later able to apply to another job. He became a community scheme director with the Scottish Football Association. This was a highly responsible role which required him to take charge of a network of community development officers throughout Scotland.

	League		Scottish Cup		League Cup	
	Apps	Goals	Apps	Goals	Apps	Goals
1978/79	16	0	2	0	–	–
1979/80	35 +1	2	2	0	4	0
1980/81	39	3	1	0	9 +1	0
1981/82	31 +3	1	1	0	6	0
1982/83	20	0	1	0	5	0
	141	6	7	0	24	0
	+4 sub. listings				+1 sub. listing	

Rikki Fleming ———————————————————————

Central defender, 1968-1978

After being released by Rangers, Rikki Fleming played for Kilwinning Rangers, although not for long. In November 1968, aged twenty-one, he signed for Ayr United. In that same month, Ayr United began a run of eleven consecutive League wins. It was difficult to get into a winning team, and his early career at Ayr involved predominantly substitute listings. His first was for a match which ended Queen's Park 0 Ayr United 3 on 4 January 1969. Fleming's first start came on 22 March 1969, a 2-1 defeat against East Stirling at Firs Park. It was a minor setback in a promotion season.

'Rikki Fleming caught the eye... Johnston got booked for fouling him and it was a reflection of the frustration running through the whole Rangers team' – Ayr United 2 Rangers 1, 13 September 1969. This incidence of Rikki Fleming doing well was not an isolated one. He was confident, cool and self-assured in defence. Although not impulsive in venturing upfield, his first Ayr

United goal eventually came in a League Cup sectional tie at home to St Mirren on 15 August 1970, a header in a 2-2 draw.

'Rikki Fleming stood out as Ayr's man of the match' – Ayr United 1 Falkirk 1, 18 November 1972. This was to develop into his best season for scoring too. He became adept at heading goals at set pieces. This is evidenced by reports stating: 'Fleming headed a Wells free-kick into the net' – Ayr United 3 East Fife 2, 10 February 1973; 'Fleming headed home a Doyle corner' – Ayr United 2 Stirling Albion 1, 24 February 1973.

On 20 March 1974, he played for the Scottish League against the Football League at Manchester City's Maine Road. In what was a successful season he had the further distinction of being named as the Supporters' Association 'Player of The Year', which he had also won in 1969/70 in his first complete senior season.

'Fleming bulleted home a tremendous header from a McCulloch corner. From the cheer which erupted you might have thought Ayr had won the Scottish Cup' – Ayr United 1 Clyde 0, 11 January 1975. The routine was familiar, albeit that he was principally a defender. Relegation from the Premier League in 1978 coincided with the release of experienced players but Rikki Fleming was not one of them despite the fact that he had by then played his last match for the club. On 26 July 1978, he was sold to Hibs for a transfer fee of £10,000. In September 1979, by which time he was with Berwick Rangers, he returned to play at Somerset Park.

	League		Scottish Cup		League Cup	
	Apps	Goals	Apps	Goals	Apps	Goals
1968/69	9 +6	0	0 +2	0	–	–
1969/70	34	0	1	0	10	0
1970/71	34	0	1	0	6	1
1971/72	11	0	0	0	3	0
1972/73	33	8	4	1	5	0
1973/74	34	1	4	1	6	0
1974/75	34	2	1	0	6	1
1975/76	30	1	3	0	6	2
1976/77	34	0	3	0	5	0
1977/78	34 +1	0	1	0	3 +1	0
	287	12	18	2	50	4
	+7 sub. listings		+2 sub. listings		+1 sub. listing	

Derek Frye
Striker, 1979-1983

Derek Frye's early career took in Kilmarnock, Stranraer and Dundee United. At Stranraer he was a sensation and this was still memorable when he joined from Dundee United in August 1979. Nicknamed 'Freddy', his debut was on 18 August 1979 against Hearts. The match was lost 4-2 but there was an opportunity to atone when the clubs were drawn together in the League Cup. A fortnight later Frye got his first Ayr United goal in the drawn home leg. Two days later Brian McLaughlin's goal put Ayr through.

Frye was direct and had a predator's instinct. His style was based around shooting whenever he was within reasonable proximity of the goalposts. In his case thirty yards was 'reasonable proximity'. In the space of a fortnight in September 1979 he scored with thirty-yard drives at Airdrie and at home to both Dunfermline and Berwick Rangers. Headers and tap-ins were also in his repertoire. As long as he was satisfying his lust for scoring, everyone at the club was happy.

He always did well in the League Cup competition. In the quarter-final in October 1980, he scored twice in a 2-2 first-leg tie at home to Hibs. George Best played for the visitors but did not impose himself. In the second leg, Frye went on as a substitute and scored the second goal in a 2-0 win which required extra time. This meant that the club had reached the semi-finals of the competition for the first time since 1969 and, at that moment, only the third time ever.

In the following season's League Cup, a sectional tie ended Partick Thistle 1 Ayr United 5. It was a substantial victory for a First Division club on a Premier League ground and was meritorious as the opposing goalkeeper was international Alan Rough. It was an amazing evening for Frye. He scored four! When the 1981/82 League campaign began, the first twelve fixtures went by undefeated. Hopes, although seemingly realistic at the time, were false. This was the dawn of a struggle that was punctuated by isolated good results.

In the final League fixture of 1982/83, a draw was required against Clyde at Shawfield in order to ensure avoiding relegation. The match was lost 3-2 but the drop was avoided because Dunfermline Athletic lost at Perth. Derek Frye scored the two Ayr goals against Clyde. He was soon to be playing his football there regularly. His transfer to Clyde took place in October 1983. With the benefit of hindsight, it can be recorded that an error of judgement was made, based on the rich vein of goalscoring form he found after the move.

On moving from Clyde, he played for Airdrie, Queen of the South and Stranraer, and in junior football with Ardrossan Winton Rovers. In the year of writing, he was assistant manager to Rowan Alexander at Gretna.

	League		Scottish Cup		League Cup	
	Apps	Goals	Apps	Goals	Apps	Goals
1979/80	37 +1	16	2	0	4	2
1980/81	25 +9	10	0 +1	0	7 +3	4
1981/82	28 +7	13	1	0	6	8
1982/83	20 +8	7	1	0	5	0
1983/84	2 +2	0	—	—	2	0
	112	46	4	0	24	14
	+27 sub. listings		+1 sub. listing		+3 sub. listings	

Billy Fulton
Inside forward, 1957-1962

Billy Fulton was a Prestwick boy who honed his skills with Ayr Albion before going to Irvine Victoria. On 28 September 1957, he was given an opportunity when he was one of the two trialists in the Ayr United forward line for a League engagement at home to Forfar Athletic. Goalkeeper Jim Fulton also made a debut in this match, the team being: J. Fulton, Thomson, Haugh, Paton, Price, Whittle, 'Junior', McMillan, Price, W. Fulton, Bradley. Billy Fulton was listed under the guise of 'Newman' and it was observed that: 'Ayr fielded a most unfamiliar looking team and it brought a strange score'. The strange score referred to was 7-4 for Ayr United and the pen of the same journalist described Fulton as 'a natural footballer'. He scored twice and was signed on the Sunday night, having already turned down Rotherham United. There was a condition that he would remain with Irvine Victoria while they were still pursuing an interest in the Scottish Junior Cup. One week later they were out!

'The rust of the rearguard stained the pretty paintwork of the front five' – Ayr United 5 Brechin City 3, 9 November 1957. This remark could have applied consistently in season 1957/58, which developed into an extravaganza of many goals both scored and conceded. Although scoring just once in that match, Billy Fulton was considered to be the star player afield.

The 1958/59 Championship season would have seen Fulton flourish, had it not been for the need to go on national service. An away win over East Fife on 29 November 1958 was his last match prior to reporting to the RAF. A posting to the Bristol area saw him guesting for Bristol City. He remained unavailable to Ayr United until the outset of season 1959/60, albeit that he was still connected to his RAF unit. A long-term injury to Alastair McIntyre resulted in Billy Fulton playing regularly at outside right during much of that season but the effect was the same. 'Fulton is putting in a tremendous amount of spirit into his play' – St Mirren 4 Ayr United 3, 28 November 1959. Yet there were fleeting reminders that he was still on national service. For example he was not released from his unit to play against Clyde at Shawfield on 17 September 1960. The reason given was that he was required for the Battle of Britain Week ceremonies. In December of that year he was demobbed.

After one season back in the Second Division, it was expected that he would move in the summer of 1962. The move took place and when Ayr United made it back into the First Division in 1966, he found himself in an opposing team while at Falkirk. In August 1970, while captain of St Mirren, he scored with a thirty-five yard drive, during a League Cup sectional tie at Ayr which ended 2-2.

On reflection it was a pity that he should have burst onto the senior scene to such great effect, only to have his Ayr United career interrupted by military service which was mandatory. The positive aspect was that his skills had not eroded during his absence.

	League		Scottish Cup		League Cup	
	Apps	Goals	Apps	Goals	Apps	Goals
1957/58	28	6	2	0	–	–
1958/59	10	2	0	0	5	0
1959/60	27	7	3	1	6	0
1960/61	31	13	2	0	4	1
1961/62	31	11	1	1	8	3
	127	39	8	2	23	4

Willie Furphy

Central defender, 1986-1992

During the 1986 close season, Ayr United signed Willie Furphy from Eastern Villa. His first-team debut was not long deferred. Stevie McIntyre was injured in a midweek Skol Cup win at Kilmarnock and the consequent reshuffle resulted in this team being named for League duty at Alloa on the Saturday: Purdie, McCann, Buchanan, McAllister, Furphy, McCracken, Wilson, Sludden, McDonald, Mauchlen, Irons. Substitutes: Gillies, Granger. The match was lost 1-0. Thereafter Stevie McIntyre returned at right-back with Jim McCann reverting to the position occupied by Willie Furphy at Alloa. Three weeks later, Jim McCann was unable to play at Stranraer due to a hamstring injury. Furphy deputised faultlessly in a scoreless draw. His performance there was replicated in the next match. From then on he was first choice.

The rigours of Second Division football were undaunting for him. Playing alongside someone of Ian McAllister's class was beneficial, although Willie Furphy was an outstanding player in his own right. His style was not based upon desperately clearing his lines. Whether on the ground or in the air, he showed creativity and composure.

During the successful title push of 1987/88, the team was rich in individual talent. Deserved publicity was accorded to the marksmen, but this team oozed quality from goalkeeper George Watson outwards. In the entire campaign, Willie Furphy missed just two League matches: Alloa Athletic away, on the day the Championship was clinched, and East Stirling at home when the trophy was presented. That cruel luck was caused by a hamstring injury.

Owing to his being a signing rebel, he missed the start of 1990/91. The club could ill-afford to lose him and it was good news when he relented. In January 1991, George Burley became player-manager. This gave rise to an unusual situation where Furphy captained with his manager on the field. Yet there was no doubt that Furphy had the authority. In a match at Kilmarnock in August 1991, he shouted at Burley for what he perceived as lack of concentration. As part of the build-up to 1991/92, Coventry City played at Somerset Park. In a match which Ayr United won 3-1, Willie Furphy put in a superb performance.

Prior to the start of 1992/93, he again found himself in a contract dispute. The uncertainty of his future caused the captaincy to be passed to Nigel Howard. Furphy had, however, put pen to paper but only on a one-month deal. At the end of August he was freed and he joined Kilmarnock on trial. His next club was Dumbarton, also on trial. A further move took him to Elgin City, then in the Highland League. In 1994/95 he was with Ross County in their first season in the Third Division. In 1999, he joined Stranraer, prior to signing for Elgin City again in September 2000, during Elgin's first season in the Third Division.

	League		Scottish Cup		League Cup	
	Apps	Goals	Apps	Goals	Apps	Goals
1986/87	35 +1	1	4	0	0	0
1987/88	37	0	4	0	2	0
1988/89	34	0	1	0	1	0
1989/90	34	0	2	0	0	0
1990/91	24	0	4	0	0	0
1991/92	39	0	2	0	3	0
1992/93	6	0	–	–	1	0
	209	1	17	0	7	0
	+1 sub. listing					

Duncan George
Midfielder 1984-1986, 1991-1997

Duncan George made his Ayr United debut before he was seventeen. He was from the club's youth system and George Caldwell elevated him to the first-team (after doing well in the reserves) after John McNiven's injury. George made his debut in a 2-1 defeat against Clyde on 17 November 1984.

The following season saw relegation and George given a free transfer. He went from Irvine Meadow to Stirling Albion to Stranraer. In March 1991, Jim McCann and Jim Hughes were transferred to Stranraer. Duncan George moved the other way, with a cash adjustment in Stranraer's favour. George Burley picked him for a 0-0 draw at Partick Thistle, and he became a regular.

He was a creative determined midfielder. In 1992, Motherwell came to Ayr in the Scottish Cup third round. They were the holders and, with three minutes left, their grip on it looked vulnerable. After Garry Agnew had driven a free-kick at the defensive wall, the ball broke to George who made it 1-1. The replay was lost but the moment was memorable.

A mid-table phase was entered, thereby creating a comfort zone that had not existed during the relegation-threatened time when George had first been at Ayr, although restructuring caused a mid-table relegation battle in 1993/94. Yet despite mid-table security, he never lacked incentive. A consequence of this was that opponents sometimes 'mixed it' with him. On 5 February 1994, he was stretchered off eight minutes into a 4-1 win at Brechin after a heavy tackle from Ralph Brand which ended his season. His next two visits to the same ground brought similar misery. On 24 August 1996 he was sent off and on 22 February 1997 he again got an early bath after a tackle on Brand.

In 1995 the club descended into the Second Division but George was retained. Celtic visited Somerset Park in the 1995/96 season in the Coca-Cola Cup. He brilliantly marked John Collins, before leaving the field with a fractured arm. Similarly, he did an effective job on Paul Gascoigne when Ayr United played Rangers in the Coca-Cola Cup at Ibrox the following season.

Duncan George's last competitive game for Ayr was a 2-0 win at Berwick at the end of 1996/97, the day when the Second Division Championship was clinched. In August 1997 he was transferred back to Stranraer and he found himself playing for the Second Division Champions in consecutive seasons.

	League		Scottish Cup		League Cup	
	Apps	Goals	Apps	Goals	Apps	Goals
1984/85	1	0	0	0	0	0
1985/86	1 +1	0	0	0	0	0
1990/91	9	0	–	–	–	–
1991/92	33	1	2	1	3	0
1992/93	37 +1	0	2	0	0	0
1993/94	17	0	1	0	1	0
1994/95	28	1	0	0	0	0
1995/96	24 +1	1	0	0	2	0
1996/97	16 +3	2	0 +1	0	2	0
	166	5	5	1	8	0
	+6 sub. listings		+1 sub. listing			

The Gibsons of Larkhall comprised a famous footballing family. Neilly Gibson, the father, had been a star player with Rangers and Scotland before and after the turn of the twentieth century. His footballing talent was inherited by three sons. Jimmy Gibson's senior career spanned Partick Thistle and Aston Villa and he was one of the 'Wembley Wizards' of 1928. Neil Gibson junior played for Clyde for a total of eleven seasons. As for Willie Gibson, the eldest brother, read on.

On 11 October 1919, Ayr United had a fixture at Motherwell. After the game, manager James MacDonald went to Larkhall to sign Willie Gibson, a wing half with St Anthony's. A fortnight later he had a first-team debut in a 1-0 home win over Hibs.

From October 1920 the policy of selecting either Hogg or Gibson was dispensed with. Hogg remained at right half while, from that point on, Gibson became regular at left half. In his initial season he would not have been considered for inclusion in that position. From the club's foundation in 1910 it had been the sacred domain of Switcher McLaughlan until that player's release in the summer of 1920. The Somerset Park regulars would have compared Gibson with McLaughlan.

Goalscoring was not his responsibility but it was inevitable that such opportunities would fall to him. His first goal came in the opening minute of a visit from Celtic on 12 March 1921. The match was won 3-1. Suitably encouraged he scored a week later in a 4-1 away victory over St Mirren.

In season 1921/22 Jimmy Gibson broke into the Partick Thistle team with the consequence that brother opposed brother. On 11 February 1922 Partick Thistle, as holders, played a second-round Scottish Cup tie at Ayr. Willie appeared in his customary left half position and Jimmy played at right

half for the Jags. Ayr United lost 1-0. At this stage the other brother, Neil Gibson junior, had not played in the senior game but he joined Clyde in 1923.

The Ayr United half-back line of Hogg, McLeod and Gibson could be rhymed off by supporters for several decades afterwards. Yet when the 1923/24 season was opened, the half-back line was Hogg, McLeod and Cunningham. That opening match was a 3-0 reverse away to Partick Thistle for whom the opening goal was scored by Jimmy Gibson. Willie Gibson's absence was easily explained. He had refused to sign a new contract. As the season progressed he remained a signing rebel. Then, in November 1923, the impasse which kept him from playing football was broken. He was sold to Newcastle United for £2,500. It was a fabulous move which brought instant success. He was in the Newcastle United team which beat Aston Villa 2-0 in the 1924 FA Cup final. Further glory manifested itself in a Football League Championship medal in 1926/27. Such achievements beg the question of why he did not gain an international cap. The answer lay in the exceptional form of Jimmy McMullan who captained Scotland.

In becoming a qualified masseur, Willie Gibson was able to maintain his links with football after his playing days had expired. He became trainer of the Welsh and Scottish international teams and at club level he served Birmingham City and Queen's Park.

	League		Ayr Charity Cup		Scottish Cup	
	Apps	Goals	Apps	Goals	Apps	Goals
1919/20	9	0	0	0	0	0
1920/21	31	2	1	0	5	0
1921/22	39	2	1	0	2	0
1922/23	38	0	1	0	3	0
	117	4	3	0	10	0

Johnny Graham
Midfielder, 1971-1976

Johnny Graham joined Third Lanark after being spotted with Strathclyde Juniors. His career later took in Dundee United, Falkirk and Hibs. His Ayr United debut was against Morton on 4 September 1971. After a 1-0 win, it was written that he was 'like a breath of fresh air.'

By the following month he was more akin to a hurricane. On 9 October 1971, a 3-1 deficit at Airdrie was transformed into a sensational 4-3 win. Johnny Graham scored all four. This four-goal feat was repeated, in the penultimate League fixture of 1971/72. Partick Thistle lost 4-0 at Somerset Park.

In the 1972/73 Scottish Cup run, Partick Thistle were defeated in the quarter-finals. Graham was the key man. The following midweek, he went off injured during a 2-0 win over Hearts, missed the next two League fixtures, and made a comeback at the Scottish Cup semi-final. He may not have been ready but his quality made his selection a justifiable gamble. He missed the second half and, today, supporters recall that beating Rangers would have been more likely with a fit Graham.

In 1973/74 he was bestowed with the club captaincy. The success of 1972/73 was built upon and the Scottish Cup semi-finals were almost reached again. In front of a 17,219 attendance, Johnny Graham's penalty kick gave the team a first-half lead in a quarter-final tie. Alan Anderson forced a replay with a goal ten minutes from the end. Somerset Park housed 16,185 for a replay in which Hearts' winner came at the end of extra time.

In 1974/75, Ayr had to finish in the First Division's top ten in order to reach the new Premier Division. On 19 April 1975, a place in the upper echelon was guaranteed with a 3-2 win at home to Dunfermline Athletic. Johnny Graham scored twice, the first a thirty-yard free-kick. He was the Supporters' Association 'Player of The Year' that season.

On 11 October 1975, he scored with a clinical volley in a 3-0 destruction of Rangers at Somerset Park. Despite this and other high profile victories, Premier League survival came down to a last-game showdown against Motherwell. Johnny Graham had been a regular fixture in his attacking midfield role but, together with Gordon Cramond, he was ruled out. In dramatic circumstances the match was won. Yet the two players just mentioned were deserving of a special acknowledgement for assisting the club into a situation where there was a fighting chance.

Before the start of 1976/77 he returned to Falkirk. In July 1978 it was prematurely announced that he was returning to Ayr as reserve team coach, as Falkirk claimed that he was still signed by them. The matter was resolved with the payment of a nominal fee. Business interests changed his focus and he became a regular spectator at Queen's Park after his son joined them.

	League		Scottish Cup		League Cup	
	Apps	Goals	Apps	Goals	Apps	Goals
1971/72	34	14	3	0	—	—
1972/73	28	7	4	0	7	3
1973/74	31	10	4	3	6	0
1974/75	29 +3	12	1	0	1 +1	0
1975/76	34 +1	16	3	0	6	3
1976/77	5 +3	3	—	—	6	1
	161	62	15	3	26	7
	+7 sub. listings				+1 sub. listing	

Ian Hawkshaw
Inside forward, 1965-1968

Although a native of Irvine, Ian Hawkshaw signed for Ayr United from St Johnstone during the 1965 close season. The worst season in the club's history had just ended. Compounding the situation was the signing policy. By scrapping the reserve team, nine players were released. The balance was far from restored by acquiring Ian Hawkshaw and Johnny Grant, a winger from Hibs. Two close-season signings to supplement a struggling squad and no reserve team! Despite the prevailing conditions, manager Tom McCreath seemed serious when he spoke about promotion being the ambition.

Ian Hawkshaw's debut came in a League Cup sectional tie at home to Stenhousemuir on 14 August 1965. He scored twice in a 5-2 win. The next sectional tie brought Montrose to Ayr. It provided two Ian Hawkshaw goals in a 5-0 victory. Even this early, it could be seen that a transformation was taking place.

In the opening League fixture, it took Ian Hawkshaw just ninety seconds to record a goal in a 3-2 away win at Montrose in midweek. Such early season successes were becoming too frequent to be defined as a temporary run of form. Hawkshaw's form made him an integral part of it all. He was possessed of an extraordinary dribbling ability. Sometimes he was criticised for being greedy. Yes, he was greedy with the ball, but it took supreme skill to afford him such a luxury. Besides, his incisive runs created goalscoring opportunities while his more superfluous dribbling was great to watch.

He received a seven-day suspension in April 1966. An end of season fixture pile up necessitated three games being missed between the specified dates. These were the only games missed by Ian Hawkshaw in the entire 1965/66 season and it was just too bad

that he missed the successful push for the Second Division Championship. On the day promotion was clinched at Arbroath, Ally MacLeod took part in a television interview in which he claimed: 'If he (Hawkshaw) parted with the ball a little sooner, he wouldn't be in my team. He would be in the Scotland team.' The reference to 'my team' was interesting. This was marginally before his job title became manager rather than coach.

After a brief stay in the First Division, the club again had the ambition of winning the Second Division Championship in 1967/68. This was not realised, although Ian Hawkshaw had the satisfaction of being Ayr's top scorer. 'Hawkshaw scored a goal that was worthy of a more illustrious occasion. Black beat his man cleverly and slipped the ball to Hawkshaw who cut into the middle and fired a great shot into the net' – Albion Rovers 0 Ayr United 2, 7 October 1967. Five minutes later he scored again. Moments later, a memorable day was finished when he was sent off! The decision was described as 'a travesty'.

In the 1968 close season, Hawkshaw was out of contract. He was also unsettled. The anticipated move took place when he joined Clydebank. His whole career comprised Kello Rovers, Saltcoats Victoria, Airdrie, Saltcoats Victoria again, St Johnstone, Ayr United, Clydebank, Montrose, East Stirling, Irvine Victoria and Hurlford United.

	League		Scottish Cup		League Cup	
	Apps	Goals	Apps	Goals	Apps	Goals
1965/66	33	14	3	0	8	4
1966/67	25 +1	4	1	0	8	3
1967/68	32	21	1	0	10	2
	90	39	5	0	26	9
	+1 sub. listing					

Bob Hepburn

Goalkeeper, 1926-1937

Bob Hepburn made his Ayr United debut after an injury to George Nisbet. 'Hep' was from Quarter, near Hamilton, and was twenty-two when signed from Dykehead of the Scottish Third Division. Straight away he faced East Fife at on 13 February 1926. From then he became first choice. Later that year, on 20 November, he made an impression at Armadale. In the course of a 4-1 defeat he was sent off for fighting. The resultant suspension caused him to miss League games against Raith Rovers and Dumbarton. Andrew Cochran deputised while Celtic's John Thomson played for Ayr United reserves on the corresponding Saturdays.

Promotion in 1928 enabled him to test his ability in the First Division. At the end of 1928/29 only Bob Hepburn and Norman Price had appeared in all the campaign's matches.

The club flirted with relegation in 1930/31 but Hepburn could not be blamed for a situation necessitating a last-game escape. 'Ayr United have a goalkeeper not far short of international class' was a response to a 5-1 defeat at Partick Thistle on 18 October 1930. His heroics were not always in vain. At the end of a scoreless draw at St Mirren on 6 December 1930, he got an ovation. In that season's Scottish Cup competition he scored! Clackmannan were brushed aside 11-2 at Somerset Park and when Pearson Ferguson was fouled for a penalty kick, Hepburn, exercising his right as captain to take it, scored with a left-foot strike.

On 5 September 1931 John Thomson, Celtic's goalkeeper, was fatally injured at Ibrox. Hepburn replaced him for Scotland in a 3-1 win over Ireland, his only international.

George Wilson became first-choice 'keeper early in 1933/34. 'Hepburn's Triumphant Return' was the headline which greeted a 1-1 draw at Hearts on the last Saturday of 1933.

On 19 September 1934, a benefit was accorded to him. Manchester City gave a fine display in their 4-1 win.

Early in 1935/36, Hep suffered knee trouble and spent time in the reserves. T. Gregg Smith, signed as an amateur from Queen's Park, became first choice, then Bob Smith was the regular custodian in 1936/37. Although still registered with Ayr, Hep played for Stranraer at this time, and was released at the end of that season.

	League Apps	Ayr Charity Cup Apps	Scottish Cup Apps
1925/26	7	1	—
1926/27	36	1	2
1927/28	38	0	2
1928/29	38	—	3
1929/30	33	2	2
1930/31	38	—	3
1931/32	37	2	2
1932/33	35	—	3
1933/34	17	0	2
1934/35	36	—	4
1935/36	17	0	1
	332	6	24

The League match versus Falkirk on 9 March 1935 was later declared void and replayed. The void match has been included in the statistics.

Being a goalkeeper, a 'Goals' column has not been included but he scored a Scottish Cup goal in 1931.

Although making no appearances, he was on Ayr United's retained list in 1936/37.

Jimmy Hogg
Wing half, 1918-1925

Jimmy Hogg was born at Springs, near Woodside, and his family moved from Ayrshire to Hamilton when he was ten. In the summer of 1918 he joined Ayr United from Vale of Clyde. Then, at the outset of 1918/19 he was immediately installed in the first team for the opening League fixture at home to Third Lanark. The match was lost 2-0.

A fortnight later a journalist noted that the supporters were 'pleased with young Hogg'. A further fortnight into his career came his first senior goal. The satisfaction was tempered by the result, a 3-1 defeat against Clyde.

Hogg was wholehearted. On New Year's Day 1919, he was uncompromising in his treatment of the great Alan Morton, then of Queen's Park. He was spoken to not only by the referee but also, sportingly, Switcher McLaughlan, his captain.

At the conclusion of his first senior season he received his first senior medal when Queen's Park were beaten for custody of the Ayr Charity Cup. He came close to realising a loftier ambition when chosen to travel to Cardiff with Scotland in February 1920.

Having been elevated to the brink of international selection there was no departure from his tough style. Following a 2-1 victory over Partick Thistle on 27 August 1921, his performance was neatly summarised: 'Hogg is always a trier but should tone down his tackling efforts a bit.' On 8 October in the same year, again in a 2-1 home win, Motherwell's Reid got sent off after being aggravated into a bad challenge. Four weeks later, during a visit from Queen's Park, an opponent called MacDonald was driven to attempt to hit him. He failed because of a pre-emptive butt from Hogg, who was sent off.

Indiscipline did not damage his international prospects. On 4 March 1922 he played for Scotland in a 2-1 win over Ireland.

Jimmy Hogg did not play for Scotland again although his club form never dipped. Neither should it be interpreted that he was capable solely of fouling. On 11 November 1922, Ayr United pulled off a spectacular 4-1 away win over Celtic. During that game he went on a solo run, beating three men before scoring.

On 5 January 1924, Rangers came to Ayr undefeated in the twenty-two League fixtures played to that point, but they lost 2-1 despite the game being refereed by a Mr Dickson from Ibrox! It is on record that 'Jimmy Hogg played a hard game'. After the match Alan Morton went into the home dressing room to offer his congratulations and to hand Hogg a donation towards his testimonial. Morton had been on the wrong end of Hogg's challenges both with Queen's Park and Rangers, besides which the Ayr man was highly disliked by the Rangers fans. It was magnificently sporting. The testimonial, played two days earlier, had drawn a small crowd of 'about 1,000'.

After 1925's relegation, Hogg was spared the Second Division by joining Clydebank on a free transfer. His career ended with the beautifully named Glenburn Blackshirts.

He lived out his life in Ayr's Lansdowne Road and died on 11 February 1974.

| | League | | Ayr Charity Cup | | Victory Cup | | Scottish Cup | |
	Apps	Goals	Apps	Goals	Apps	Goals	Apps	Goals
1918/19	32	2	1	0	1	0	—	—
1919/20	35	1	1	0	—	—	3	0
1920/21	39	1	1	0	—	—	5	0
1921/22	39	0	1	0	—	—	2	0
1922/23	32	1	1	0	—	—	3	0
1923/24	36	1	0	0	—	—	7	0
1924/25	17	1	0	0	—	—	2	0
	230	7	5	0	1	0	22	0

Gregg Hood

Central defender, 1991-1998

For a First Division fixture at Forfar on 20 April 1991, Gregg Hood, aged sixteen, was an unused substitute. It was a day of anger. George Burley was sent off and an injury-time penalty was conceded from which Forfar made it 1-1. It would be understating matters to say refereeing caused the mood.

He was tried in pre-season friendlies in 1991 and it was felt that he would break through. On 12 October 1991, aged seventeen, he was in the starting line-up against Forfar Athletic, a 4-0 win. A week later he started in a 3-2 defeat at Clydebank. These were his only competitive starts of 1991/92. However he was being nurtured in John Connolly's youth team. They contested the final of the BP Youth Cup in April 1992, but a 2-0 defeat was inflicted by Hibs at Easter Road. Hood and Derek Allan were standouts.

From March 1993, Hood became a first-team regular, although appearances were curtailed by injury. It is remarkable to relate that he feared being freed in 1992/93. That was not even a possibility. He was recognised at Scotland Under-21 level, winning 3 caps.

He was very good in the air and began to use this in attack. On 4 January 1994, he scored a headed goal from a corner in a 2-0 win at Clydebank, Four days later, in a 1-1 draw with Dumbarton, he again headed home. Then, on 22 January, in a 3-1 win over Stirling Albion he headed a further goal. These games were all in the first five of Simon Stainrod's reign as manager.

In the summer of 1994 he was a contract rebel. Perhaps he knew what lay ahead! On consecutive Saturdays straddling November and December 1994, he scored in 1-1 draws (Dundee away, Raith Rovers home). Alas, consistent defeats became monotonous. Hood belonged on a better stage.

He missed much of 1995/96 through injury. A substitute appearance at Clyde marked a return in October 1995 but he broke his arm in a training-ground accident. His next comeback was in a 1-0 win at Montrose on 13 January 1996 but he had to have stitches. In 1996/97 he again missed matches prior to returning when the push towards the Second Division Championship was being mounted. He played at Berwick the day it was clinched.

At the end of 1997/98 he was released. He was the club's longest-serving player. In January 1999 he joined Partick Thistle.

	League		Scottish Cup		League Cup	
	Apps	Goals	Apps	Goals	Apps	Goals
1990/91	0 +2	0	—	—	—	—
1991/92	2 +8	0	0	0	0	0
1992/93	12 +4	1	0	0	0 +1	0
1993/94	26 +2	3	1	0	0	0
1994/95	15 +1	3	0	0	0	0
1995/96	17 +1	2	0	0	0	0
1996/97	18 +2	1	1	0	3	1
1997/98	11 +3	1	0	0	1	0
	101	11	2	0	4	1
	+23 sub. listings				+1 sub. listing	

On the evening of 12 November 1996, a scattering of spectators turned up at Somerset Park to watch the reserves play their Airdrie counterparts. The Ayr team included trialist Alain Horace. Born in Madagascar, he had French citizenship and was formerly with Mulhouse (France). This was an unusual background for a player who had come to these shores for trials with Hartlepool United and Motherwell. He had played for Motherwell in a reserve fixture against Hibs but manager Alex McLeish did not pursue an interest. At Ayr he was an instant star.

Horace went straight into the first team for a Second Division fixture at Stranraer on the Saturday. He was one of two twenty-four-year-olds to make an Ayr United debut in that team. The other one was Mark Humphries. The frustrating match was more than compensated for by a brilliant display. Horace's skills were tremendous and he immediately became a talking point. He scored directly from a corner kick for the only goal and had to disentangle himself from fans.

The quest for promotion became a three-way fight between Ayr United, Hamilton Accies and Livingston. 'Alain Horace ran the show in midfield' – Dumbarton 1 Ayr United 1, 18 January 1997. This was tantamount to a normal game for him. The fans just loved to sing repeated choruses of 'Bonjour Alain Horace'. Brilliant display followed brilliant display and these choruses became well aired.

On 19 April 1997, a 1-1 draw away to Clyde was sufficient to guarantee promotion. Three matches remained, the next being Hamilton Accies away. Ayr United had a one-point lead over Hamilton, although the Accies had a better goal difference. It was considered that a point would be satisfactory from the fixture. At this time, Hamilton ground-shared with Albion Rovers but, in order to accommodate the expected crowd, the fixture was moved to Motherwell's Fir Park. Before the match, there was an incident which amply illustrated Horace's popularity. In the warm-up, the Ayr players conducted an exercise which involved running across the pitch. The bulk of the Ayr support was in the stand opposite the main stand and, when Horace reached the touchline on that side, he was given a standing ovation! The match ended 1-1 and, after a 2-0 win over Brechin, the title was won with a 2-0 victory at Berwick; a victory in which he scored.

That summer, he damaged a knee during pre-season training. It required a cruciate ligament operation and it was forecast that he could miss the entire season. This was sickeningly true. Nine minutes of involvement in an Ayrshire Cup tie at Kilmarnock was hardly a comeback.

In July 1998, he did play during the club's tour to Sweden and, in a pre-season friendly at home to Walsall, he appeared for sixty-four minutes. His recovery was far from complete though. Between December 1998 and early January 1999, he went on as a substitute in four consecutive First Division fixtures. Sadly, he was released at the end of that season. He returned to France with a view to playing at a lower level in order to build up his fitness in the hope of returning to the French League.

	League		Scottish Cup		League Cup	
	Apps	Goals	Apps	Goals	Apps	Goals
1996/97	21 +1	5	1	0	–	–
1997/98	0	0	0	0	0	0
1998/99	0 +4	0	0	0	0	0
	21	5	1	0	0	0
	+5 sub. listings					

John Hughes

Central defender, 2000-2002

'Yogi' was a 'man mountain' of a defender who had the reputation of being a formidable opponent. At the outset, he was a junior player with Newtongrange Star before breaking into the senior game with Berwick Rangers. Berwick sold him on to Swansea City and, in turn, he was further sold on to Falkirk. His next clubs were Celtic then Hibs. On signing for Ayr United in the 2000 close season, he had captained Hibs the previous season. Gordon Dalziel, his new manager, said: 'I worked very hard to get Hughes and thought at the weekend I had lost him when I heard of all the clubs who were in. He will be a phenomenal signing for us.'

Intensive signing activity compounded the importance of the tour to Sweden in July 2000. The process of becoming an efficient playing unit was assisted by the circumstances. Hughes had three of his Hibs teammates of the previous season for company, whereas new strikers Eddie Annand and James Grady had been playing together at Dundee.

Yogi was immediately made club captain, although it was unfortunate that he was to be afflicted by injury in the season ahead. At Livingston, on 9 September 2000, the day he turned thirty-six, it was necessary for him to be substituted after less than half an hour by the hitherto unknown Mohammed Benlaredj. A hamstring problem had rendered him doubtful before the match and his selection amounted to a failed gamble. The problem persisted and, after his return, there was the irritation of a three-match ban in November.

His first goal in an Ayr shirt was on 6 January 2001. Four days earlier, a 6-0 win had been recorded against Morton at Cappielow Park and it was expected that the scoring momentum would see Clyde beaten. With ten minutes remaining, the game was scoreless. Then John Hughes struck at the Somerset Road end with a header. A late James Grady goal sealed it at 2-0. In February, Yogi sustained cracked ribs during training. This was so severe that he did not return until the final League match of the season.

Season 2001/02 was the one in which he really made his reputation as an Ayr United great. It all began to go spectacularly right on 26 January 2002, when Dunfermline Athletic were soundly beaten 3-0 at Ayr in a fourth-round Scottish Cup tie. Eleven days later came the CIS Cup semi-final against Hibs at Hampden. Eleven minutes into extra time, the illuminated scoreboards momentarily flickered to show an amended score of Hibs 0 Ayr United 1. To the supporters, the excitement was tempered by a sense of panic ranging from mild to acute depending on the temperament of the individual. In the entire history of the club, no Ayr United team had ever reached a major cup final. The major concern was whether the scoreline would remain intact. On the field, it was a time for steady nerves and defending. John Hughes lived up to his 'man mountain' reputation and the final whistle was blown with no further scoring. At the end, he had a huge grin which encapsulated the mood. In contentious circumstances, the final was lost to Rangers but John Hughes became the first player ever to lead Ayr United out for a major final.

In the close season he returned to Falkirk. Then, during 2002/03, he was appointed joint manager with Owen Coyle. Both of them combined playing with management and by the conclusion of that season they had steered Falkirk to the First Division Championship.

| | League | | Scottish Cup | | League Cup | |
	Apps	Goals	Apps	Goals	Apps	Goals
2000/01	18 +2	1	1	0	1	0
2001/02	30	1	5	0	5	0
	48 +2 sub. listings	2	6	0	6	0

Between the ages of six and sixteen, Glynn Hurst lived in South Africa. He then returned to England to sign for Tottenham Hotspur. Thereafter he was with Barnsley and had loan spells with Swansea City and Mansfield Town. His next move was to Emley, a Yorkshire non-League club which had an outstanding FA Cup run in 1997/98. Ultimately, he was in their team on the occasion of being eliminated by West Ham United, of the Premiership, at Upton Park, the margin being a slender 2-1. At the age of twenty-two, he was transferred to Ayr United in March 1998. The fee was £30,000.

After getting hurt in training, he did not play for the club until the start of the following season. At that point, his impact was immediate. Pacy strikers with an explosive shot are a rarity. Glynn Hurst fitted that profile and the fans were soon singing his name. Hurst had a smile which seemed to fill his face, especially after scoring.

His first Ayr United appearances were in Sweden. On 8 August 1998, he got his first competitive goal for the club on the occasion of a 3-1 win away to St Mirren in a League Cup tie. Even this early there was strong evidence that he would form a potent strike force with Andy Walker.

On the evening of 18 August 1998, in the next round of the League Cup, Hurst scored at Motherwell. The goal was timed at twenty-two seconds. It was a club record with one second to spare, albeit that Neil Tarrant was to establish a new record by scoring after twenty seconds in February 2000. The Motherwell tie was won 2-0 and there was a warning that Ayr United in general and Hurst in particular, would have a good season.

On 19 December 1998, Gordon Dalziel planned his team without Hurst who had an ankle problem. On the morning of the match the player was optimistic to the extent that he

was given a fitness test. He went on to score a hat-trick in a 5-0 rout of Hamilton Accies. By this time he had former Emley teammate Mickey Reynolds with him on the team.

One of Hurst's finest matches was a Scottish Cup tie in which he did not score. The occasion was a third-round visit from Kilmarnock in 1999. He was involved in setting up the first goal and was brought down for the penalty kick which resulted in the second goal of the 3-0 win. The trademark Hurst smile was heavily evident at the end.

At the end of 1998/99, Hurst was the club's highest League scorer since Brian McLaughlin in 1978/79. In September 1999, he signed a three-year contract. Although he did not see out that contract he continued to excite the fans. There were team selections in 1999/00 which indicated that League points were sacrificed in order to keep key players fresh for impending Scottish Cup ties. By the following season, the League challenge was back on track and so was the scoring momentum of Glynn Hurst. On 2 January 2001, he scored five in a 6-0 away win over Morton. It was the first time an Ayr United player had scored five in a competitive fixture since Peter Price on 26 November 1955. Yet there was no secret that Hurst wished to return to England. On 15 February 2001 he was sold to Stockport County for £150,000. After appearing in twenty-five matches, £25,000 more was received. In December 2001 he joined Chesterfield and a further move took him to Notts County in the summer of 2004.

| | League | | Scottish Cup | | League Cup | |
	Apps	Goals	Apps	Goals	Apps	Goals
1998/99	34	18	4	0	4	2
1999/00	26	14	5	0	1	0
2000/01	19	17	1	0	1	0
	79	49	10	0	6	2

As early as 1963, Alex Ingram played, and won, at Somerset Park, while with Queen's Park. In the summer of 1966 he left that club to sign for Ayr United. He was to develop into one of Scottish football's hard men. His fearless style sometimes made him look like a casualty of war.

His initial season at Ayr was a bad one for everybody connected to Ayr United, yet there were still references to his heading ability. With the club back in the Second Division in 1967/68, 'Dixie' really began to assert himself. The momentum rolled into the 1968/69 promotion season when he was the top scorer at the club. In October 1968, it was reported that a five-figure offer from Falkirk had been turned down. This would prove wise. 'Alex Ingram did not score but still emerged as the best player afield' – Ayr United 4 Montrose 0, 2 January 1969. Dixie imposed himself so much in the penalty area, that his teammates were able to take advantage of flicks, ricochets and knockdowns. 'Alex Ingram was booked a few minutes after the start for barging into Queen's Park goalkeeper John Taylor. Ingram has a big heart but the fans will not endorse this type of foul' – Queen's Park 0 Ayr United 3, 4 January 1969. In this case the victim was

an Ayr boy who was to attend Somerset Park as a spectator in later years. Yet the scribe was partly wrong in his opinion of how the fans would perceive Dixie. To the regular supporters he could do nothing wrong. On the evening of 23 April 1969, in the course of a 1-1 draw at home to Motherwell, visiting full-back Whiteford scored an own goal while under pressure from Alex Ingram. This was reminiscent of 23 November 1968, at Stranraer, when centre half Hannah scored an own goal from forty yards while being harassed by Dixie.

In November 1969, he played for the Scottish League against the Irish League at Ibrox. Then, on 20 December, news emerged that he had been sold to Nottingham Forest for £40,000. Discreet negotiations had been ongoing since October.

In the closing days of 1970, a deal was struck whereby Ayr United agreed to pay £15,000 to bring him home. On New Year's Day 1971, he returned for a home match against Morton. After six minutes he scored in a 2-1 win.

'Alex Ingram rose high above the defence to head-flick a great goal under the crossbar from a free-kick' – Ayr United 2 Rangers 1, 2 September 1972. This was a stereotypical Ingram goal. Courage in the air, allied to timing and accuracy, made a lethal combination. Season 1972/73 was an excellent one. League points were piled on and the club had an outstanding Scottish Cup run. It is slightly unconventional for a striker to be a captain but Dixie had that role at this time. He led by example.

On 4 April 1973, Ayr United contested a Scottish Cup semi-final for the first time in the club's history. The occasion was a meeting with Rangers at Hampden and there was a sensational start. Inside the first minute, Dixie headed home a Davy Wells free-kick. Dixie's effort was ruled offside by a dubious hairline decision and the tie was eventually lost 2-0. That summer he scored eleven goals on a club tour to Newfoundland. Early in the 1973/74 season he suffered an injury in a League Cup sectional tie away to Morton. Quite apart from the threat to his goalscoring momentum, there was the further threat of staving off competition for a place once fit. Alex Ferguson was signed from Falkirk in September and other players with finishing qualities were Johnny Graham and George McLean. In mid-September, injury compelled him to be substituted in a game at Dumbarton. Two months elapsed before Dixie next made it into the starting line-up and it was a scoring return in a 1-1 draw at Arbroath.

'Ayr United won with a flash of the Dixie of old' – Ayr United 2 Hearts 1, 20 April 1974. Naturally this was a reference to a headed winner. 'Dixie walked off Boghead looking like a war casualty' – Dumbarton 1 Ayr United 2, 16 November 1974. His appetite for the game remained undiminished.

On 30 August 1975, the first batch of matches took place in Scotland's new Premier Division. One of those matches was Motherwell v. Ayr United and, since it kicked off slightly before the scheduled three o'clock kick-off time, it can reasonably be claimed that Alex Ingram was the first player ever to kick a ball in that League. The result was a 1-1 draw.

Dixie was released at the end of season 1976/77 and he went on to achieve great success by expanding his car dealerships.

He still holds the record of having scored more Scottish Cup goals for the club than any other player. In terms of all competitive goals, he remains the club's fourth highest goalscorer of all time.

	League		Scottish Cup		League Cup	
	Apps	Goals	Apps	Goals	Apps	Goals
1966/67	23 +3	4	1	0	7	4
1967/68	35	16	1	0	9	6
1968/69	36	23	2	1	8	2
1969/70	15	7	–	–	10	5
1970/71	16	4	1	0	–	–
1971/72	23 +4	5	2 +1	1	4	0
1972/73	32	5	4	3	8	2
1973/74	18 +7	3	0 +4	0	4 +1	0
1974/75	26 +4	8	1	1	5	2
1975/76	31 +1	5	3	5	6	2
1976/77	6 +10	2	0 +1	0	3 +1	1
	261	82	15	11	64	24
	+29 sub. listings		+6 sub. listings		+2 sub. listings	

Willie Japp's senior career began with Falkirk and East Stirling. Following his transfer to Ayr United he made a debut in a 2-0 win over Queen of the South on 9 December 1950 and he was described as 'a smash hit'. With Japp on the right wing and Alec Beattie on the left, the potential existed to run more than 'B' Division defences ragged. The visit of First Division Motherwell to Ayr for a Scottish Cup quarter-final tie, on 10 March 1951, brought forth a comment that: 'Willie Japp was the lad who brought cheer upon cheer to raw Ayr throats as he brought panic to the visitors' defence.' It was rough justice that the tie was lost after a replay.

Ball-playing wingers with skill had a price to pay and Japp was not immune to desperate challenges. On the last Saturday in 1951, Ayr United and St Johnstone shared six goals at Somerset Park. While making it 3-1, Japp met the joint force of St Johnstone's Christie and Innes, and had to be stretchered off.

On the evening of 13 August 1952, Dumbarton were blown away 11-1 in a League Cup sectional tie. Japp's hat-trick was eclipsed by Jim Fraser's four goals. However, on the occasion of a 4-0 League win, away to Dundee United on 15 November that year, his hat-trick captured more focus. But 30 October 1954 was a bad day. Despite the early date, Ayr United hosted a fourth-round Scottish Cup replay against Cowdenbeath. Five minutes into the second half, he was carried off but later returned to the wing. Although lame, he managed to score the final goal of the match to make it 3-3. Ayr United won the second replay. The severity of the injury kept him out until the penultimate Saturday of January 1955.

In the 1955 close season, Willie Japp was placed on the transfer list after refusing terms. This caused him to miss the start of the season ahead but he relented. At least, he relented in the matter of agreeing terms! He still wished to remain transfer-listed. The club had declined a bid from Stirling Albion.

'Willie Japp reappeared... He was as lively as a cricket' – Alloa Athletic 1 Ayr United 2, 10 September 1955. He returned with a vengeance. 'Saturday saw no respite for Ayr, for Third Lanark... made no secret by their play that they were intent on collaring the points' – Ayr United 1 Third Lanark 0, 1 October 1955. Twelve minutes from the end, Japp had scored with a mishit shot. He entered folklore with a different mishit goal.

Newly promoted Ayr United struggled to make an impression on returning to the First Division yet there was an historic victory on 12 January 1957. While holding Rangers in a hitherto scoreless match, Ayr United mustered an attack with ten minutes left. Willie Japp half-hit the ball with his left foot, only for it to hit a hard patch and soar in for the only goal. Thereafter he played just three more first-team matches before a transfer request ensured that he would never again play for Ayr competitively. Yet it took until November before he rejoined East Stirling. He next played for Berwick Rangers.

| | League | | Scottish Cup | | League Cup | |
	Apps	Goals	Apps	Goals	Apps	Goals
1950/51	19	6	4	0	–	–
1951/52	24	5	1	0	3	1
1952/53	27	8	2	2	6	4
1953/54	27	6	1	1	8	1
1954/55	17	1	4	1	8	1
1955/56	31	9	2	0	0	0
1956/57	19	3	1	0	6	4
1957/58	0	0	–	–	0	0
	164	38	15	4	31	11

Johnny Kilgannon
Inside forward, 1962-1964

Aged twenty-six, Johnny Kilgannon joined Ayr United from Stirling Albion in summer 1962. His earlier clubs had been Stenhousemuir and Luton Town. The 1962/63 season opened with a League Cup sectional tie, away to East Stirling but, owing to a family bereavement, his debut was deferred until the next match. That too was a League Cup sectional tie, against Berwick Rangers. In the course of a 2-2 draw, Kilgannon scored and it was a classic case of starting as he intended to continue.

That season's opening League fixture had to be approached with trepidation. St Johnstone away was potentially as tough as it could get since the host club had been relegated to the Second Division on goal average after failing to get the one point required for safety on the final day. This was hardly surprising, since visitors Dundee were in pursuit of the Championship and their 3-0 win at Perth put the issue beyond doubt. Although St Johnstone did win the Second Division title in 1962/63, Ayr United took full points off them including a 2-1 win in the opener in which Johnny Kilgannon scored.

'The acquisition of inside forward Kilgannon was the smartest piece of work in the managerial career of Gerry Mays at Somerset Park. And that's a fact. Any doubts there might have been about the bustling inside man's worth were decisively ended at Coatbridge on Saturday. Albion Rovers will endorse that finding. Kilgannon was the United spearhead whom Rovers never quite contained. He scored twice, made a third and was unlucky on different occasions not to meet with more success' – Albion Rovers 0 Ayr United 3, 29 September 1962. That win meant that Ayr United were in second place in the League. Disappointingly results then began to degenerate, although it may seem contradictory to relate that Johnny

Kilgannon's good form continued. He was ably assisted by Sandy Jones, a nineteen-year-old centre forward who was released by Motherwell and put pen to paper for Ayr United on 9 November 1962. One day later, Jones scored in the first minute of his debut at Hamilton. Jones and Kilgannon became a potent strike force in an otherwise struggling team. They totalled twenty-seven League goals between them despite finishing in thirteenth place in the Second Division. Season 1963/64 brought a finishing place of fourteenth, even although Kilgannon amassed 24 League goals. Apart from Peter Price, no Ayr United player had scored as many League goals in a season since Malky Morrison in 1945/46.

'Kilgannon crashed home a glorious winner in the eighty-ninth minute' – Ayr United 3 Stenhousemuir 2, 30 November, 1963. This was one of the all too few occasions when Kilgannon's marksmanship served a more useful purpose than narrowing the margin of defeat. Another such occasion was on 15 February 1964 when, with three minutes remaining, he scored the goal which gave Ayr United a totally unexpected 2-1 win at Aberdeen in the third round of the Scottish Cup. Successes were isolated and only seven players were retained at the end of the season. Johnny Kilgannon was one of them but his career at the club was at an end anyway and he was transferred to Dunfermline Athletic.

In February 1967, by which time he was a St Johnstone player, he died from injuries received in a road accident.

	League		Scottish Cup		League Cup	
	Apps	Goals	Apps	Goals	Apps	Goals
1962/63	35	14	1	1	4	3
1963/64	35	24	4	2	6	4
	70	38	5	3	10	7

On 26 March 1949, Sam Leckie, then of Newton Rovers, played a trial for Ayr United reserves in a Somerset Park friendly against a Rangers eleven. It ended in a 3-3 draw in which he played at left-back. If he had been at right-back, where he was also adept, he would have been in direct opposition to Tom Sutherland who, decades later, was one of the Beirut hostages who spent six years in captivity! A week after that match, Ayr United travelled to play Hamilton Accies in the League and regular left-back Joe Coupland was injured. His place was taken by Sam Leckie. The result was a creditable 1-1 draw. A week later Leckie was back at his junior club but in the last week of that month, Ayr embarked on a Highland tour, Leckie included. On the strength of his displays on tour, manager Archie Anderson signed him.

Sam Leckie played in both full-back positions for Ayr United. The opinion of one journalist implied that the player revelled in the new-found permanency in his selection. 'Sam Leckie had an argument with a tractor starting-handle earlier in the week' Suitably undaunted, he was still able to play in a 2-1 Scottish Cup win at Stirling on 27 January 1951. The perils of part-time football!

Sam Leckie, Ross Henderson, Bobby Thomson, Willie Fraser and Joe McKeown all shared the number two shirt in 1951/52. On 3 May 1952, the Ayr Charity Cup was temporarily revived to commemorate 750 years of Ayr being a Royal Burgh. That Ayr United beat Queen's Park 2-1 is not especially remarkable. A more interesting fact is that Leckie went on as a substitute. At a competitive level, substitutions were not introduced to Scottish football until 1966.

From, and including, 1952/53, he missed just four League matches over the course of four consecutive seasons. He even produced a goal from a forty-yard free-kick during a 4-3 win against Albion Rovers on 21 March 1953. It was his only competitive goal for the club and the joy was tempered by the own goal he conceded later in the same match. But it was of little avail that he was not a prolific scorer!

In September 1953, Ayr United played Rangers over two legs in the League Cup quarter-finals. Prior to the first leg at Ibrox, it was considered that Sam Leckie had the hardest job, attempting to contain Willie Waddell. A clue about his success was contained in the opinion of a writer: 'He kept Waddell reasonably quiet after settling down'.

In 1954/55, Sam Leckie appeared in every League fixture although, given the overall situation, it was a fraught time. One season later he was again an ever-present in the League and there was a palpable difference. Promotion was won in a last-game win over Brechin City in which Leckie imposed himself to great effect when the team was lacking cohesion early in the match. As if to illustrate the fickle nature of football, he made just one League appearance in the First Division. Thus ended the Ayr United career of a player nicknamed 'The Provost'.

| | League | | Scottish Cup | | League Cup | |
	Apps	Goals	Apps	Goals	Apps	Goals
1948/49	1	0	–	–	–	–
1949/50	7	0	0	0	3	0
1950/51	22	0	4	0	0	0
1951/52	6	0	0	0	1	0
1952/53	27	1	2	0	0	0
1953/54	29	0	1	0	2	0
1954/55	30	0	5	0	8	0
1955/56	36	0	2	0	5	0
1956/57	1	0	0	0	4	0
	159	1	14	0	23	0

Paul Lovering
Left-back, 2000-2003

In October 1998, Hibs paid Clydebank £120,000 for Paul Lovering but Ayr United were involved in the bidding. During the 2000 close season Lovering, then aged twenty-four, at last joined Ayr United. So did some of his teammates at Hibs! John Hughes, Michael Renwick and Pat McGinlay all moved from Hibs to Ayr that summer.

Paul Lovering's earliest games for Ayr were played in Sweden. His competitive debut was against Ross County on 5 August 2000. It was a tough match which was won 1-0 against a team suffering from two red cards; the kind of game that Lovering thrived on. Combative matches require combative players and he fitted that profile – strong in the tackle, strong on the overlap and with a good work ethic! In the club's history, Paul Lovering does not have exclusive rights to that description. He is simply one of the great Ayr United full-backs.

On 3 February 2001, he scored with a header in a 2-2 draw with Airdrie. It transpired that his next goal was also a header against Airdrie (on 18 August in the same year). However he was a useful provider of goals by virtue of his corner technique. Incisive runs culminating in dangerous cutbacks and crosses created further danger.

Lovering was useful as a central defender when called upon to fill that role. That is what happened on 8 September 2001, in the course of a game against Partick Thistle at Firhill. Mark Campbell and David Craig were already out injured, and Neil Duffy hobbled off with a groin strain. Paul Lovering then moved into a central defensive partnership alongside John Hughes and John Robertson. Although effective, it did restrict his style. He relished the freedom to pound up and down the left flank. On one occasion he came close to scoring from a range of nearly fifty yards. During a 2-1 win at Airdrie on 9 February

2002, he seized on a clearance and hit an effort that goalkeeper Bennett managed to touch over the bar.

In the 2002 CIS Cup final, he almost scored in the second minute. In anticipation of a sensational opener, the Ayr fans rose to their feet as Lovering closed in on goal. His shot went just wide. A key incident in that match also involved him. Two minutes into the second half, with Rangers leading 1-0, his former Hibs teammate Russell Latapy went down of his own propulsion. From his vantage point, the referee deemed that Lovering had fouled him but there had been insufficient contact. The resultant penalty kick put the tie beyond reach.

In the course of a 2-1 win at home to Ross County on 17 August 2002, he broke his collarbone. Despite the extent of the injury, he missed just three matches. The recovery was doubtlessly aided by his willingness to see match action again. The comeback was in a 1-0 win at Alloa in which he was red-carded!

By now, Ayr United had two raiding full-backs, the other one being Willie Lyle on the right. Lyle established himself as the club's fastest player. During the 2003 close season Paul Lovering joined St Johnstone. His next move was to Airdrie United in January 2004.

	League		Scottish Cup		League Cup	
	Apps	Goals	Apps	Goals	Apps	Goals
2000/01	21 +13	1	1	0	1	0
2001/02	27 +5	1	5	0	5	0
2002/03	21 +1	1	2	0	1	0
	69	3	8	0	7	0
	+19 sub. listings					

Ally MacLeod is assuredly the greatest of the Ayr United greats. As a player, his career took him from Third Lanark to St Mirren to Blackburn Rovers to Hibs and to Third Lanark again before joining Ayr United in the 1964 close season. He had played for Blackburn Rovers in the 1960 FA Cup final, but he was destined to make a return to big time football.

Ally was immediately installed with the Ayr United captaincy and there were glimpses of his former skills. 'MacLeod is a crowd delighter; his tanner-ba' dribbles draw cheers from the crowd and he is also perhaps the most constructive half-back in the Second Division' – Ayr United 3 Dumbarton 0, 19 September 1964. Yet, as evidenced by his number of appearances, the Ayr public saw little of these skills. He had a far more important role at the club, in the field of coaching.

Season 1964/65 remains the worst ever in the history of Ayr United. Finishing second from the foot of the Second Division brought the indignity of having to apply for re-election to the League. In the 1965 close season, the only significant signings were Johnny Grant and Ian Hawkshaw but, nevertheless, the Second Division Championship was won in the year ahead. Manager Tom McCreath stated: 'With virtually the same staff we have taken the club from the bottom five (sic) right to the top'. He also praised Ally MacLeod's contribution. McCreath had no previous experience in

senior football, therefore the conclusion can be drawn that Ally MacLeod had been responsible for some major input in that success. In suitable recognition, he was appointed club manager on 5 May 1966.

The sudden propulsion to the top meant that the club was largely unprepared for the rigours of First Division football. Back in the Second Division in 1967/68, Ally began to lay the foundations of a great era. In 1966, Ayr United had won the title with 53 points. The same haul in 1968/69 brought a runners-up spot, but that was still good enough for promotion. Ally was determined that the trauma of 1966/67 would not be repeated.

Success was built on morale. Ally MacLeod was a super optimist and he instilled a high level of self-belief into what was still a part-time squad. The opening League match of the 1969/70 season, saw Hibs crushed 3-0 at Somerset Park. Then, on 13 September 1969, the ground record was broken on an afternoon when Ayr United beat Rangers 2-1. It was the beginning of a sequence in which Rangers lost all but one League fixture played at Ayr, over the course of four consecutive seasons. On 8 October 1969, six goals were shared against Celtic who were on course for that season's European Cup final. The occasion was the League Cup semi-final which was harshly and narrowly lost in a replay. These all comprised amazing performances from players who continued to make a living outside of football. Ally milked such successes by praising his players to the hilt and ensuring that Ayr United would be back-page news at any opportunity.

He had a superb manner for dealing with defeat. A typical response to losing in, for example, October, would be that October had never been an especially good month for results anyway and November had always been better. Of course the next match would be on the first Saturday in November. He filled the players with belief as well as the fans. This was not futile optimism since these were good times.

In 1972/73, the club reached the semi-finals of the Scottish Cup for the first time ever. Combined with a League placing of sixth, it was correctly considered to be the best season in living memory. Relegation battles were banished to the past. In the whole of 1973 only Celtic and Rangers had League wins at Somerset Park and the latter only achieved it with a winner two minutes from the end on the last Saturday of the year.

League restructuring saw the birth of a ten-club Premier League in 1975/76 and some of the early season results suggested that there would be no discernible threat to Ayr United. On 11 October 1975, Rangers were beaten 3-0 at Somerset Park and, indirectly, a heavy price was paid for victory. On 4 November 1975, the board agreed to release Ally MacLeod, in order that he could become the manager of Aberdeen. That date was a Tuesday but he was permitted to take charge of the Ayr United team that night, for an Ayrshire Cup tie which was won 3-0 at Kilmarnock. At this time Ayr United had a higher League position than Aberdeen, a situation which was still intact at the season's end. In 1976/77 he won the League Cup with Aberdeen and he was manager of Scotland by the time that season had expired.

During his reign as Scotland manager, there was a public enthusiasm for the national team which has not been remotely matched ever since. Then, in September 1978, he resigned from the Scotland job in order to return to Ayr United to replace Alex Stuart as manager. Ally's first game of his second spell in charge was a First Division fixture in which Arbroath were beaten 3-0. That was on the evening of 27 September. On 12 December that year, it came as a shock when it was announced that he had agreed to become manager of Motherwell.

He later managed Airdrie before returning to Ayr for a further spell in charge. The announcement to that effect was made on 1 November 1985. By this time the club was fighting unsuccessfully to avoid the drop to the Second Division. It took two seasons to get back into the First Division and it is pleasing to record that the Second Division

The cover from the Order of Service at Ally's funeral.

Championship of 1987/88 was won with attacking abandon. The club-record points total (at two points for a win) was created in that season, and it was just like the old times with fans yearning for Saturdays. The *Daily Record* offered a crate of champagne to the first team to score 100 competitive goals that season. On beating Stranraer 3-1 at Somerset Park, on 9 April 1988, the prize was won by Ayr United. In typical fashion, Ally MacLeod offered to match the prize if the total could be taken to 150. There were four games left!

In December 1990 he resigned. His three terms of management at the club totalled close to fifteen years. To date that span is more than double that of his nearest rival. He totalled 214 League wins during these spells and again there are not even any close rivals.

His last job in management was with Queen of the South. Afterwards he became a regular attendee of Ayr United matches. At the age of seventy-two, after battling against Alzheimer's disease, he passed away on 1 February 2004.

| | League | | Scottish Cup | | League Cup | |
	Apps	Goals	Apps	Goals	Apps	Goals
1964/65	12	0	1	0	6	0

Dick Malone

Right-back, 1964-1970

After having played for Carfin Amateurs then Shotts Bon Accord, Dick Malone signed for Ayr United in the 1964 close season when he was approaching the age of seventeen. His date of birth was 22 August 1947. It is interesting to relate that his brother Frank was registered with Kilmarnock. Dick had age on his side and this was perhaps why he was not immediately installed at right-back. In the early part of 1964/65, that position was occupied by Adam Thomson, Dick Grant, John Milton, Drew Nelson, Adam Thomson again and John Milton again. During this phase he played one match at centre half to deputise for Eddie Monan. Centre half was not his natural position and his eventual selection at right-back came when Ayr United were bottom of the Second Division. The date was 31 October 1964 and it ended in a 4-0 defeat against Raith Rovers. The merry-go-round of right-backs began again, but when he next got a chance he was retained.

In the Second Division Championship season of 1965/66, he forged a reputation for being brilliant on the overlap but there was no such freedom in the aberration which comprised Ayr United's First Division campaign in 1966/67. The lowest point came when he was sent off in a Scottish Cup tie at Elgin. Aggravating the situation was the fact that the referee then called him back to administer a further booking for remarks made. These offences brought a twenty-eight-day suspension. Things could only get better and that was just how it worked out.

During the following season an offer from Clyde was received by the club and an approach was made by Fulham. The club rejected the Clyde bid and the player turned down Fulham after travelling to London to talk to their manager, Vic Buckingham. Suitably settled at Ayr, he became ever more proficient with his incisive runs. On 2 December 1967, he ran half the length of the field to score in a 3-1 win at Alloa. To this point of the season he had also shown a proficiency for scoring from free-kicks.

On 19 October 1968, he created a club record by scoring a hat-trick in a 7-1 win at home to Stenhousemuir. He remains the only Ayr United player to achieve this feat in a competitive match while playing at full-back. Only one of his three strikes came from a penalty kick. In February 1969, Ally MacLeod started to implement the idea of pushing Malone up to outside right, albeit in matches which he commenced at right-back.

Top-flight football in 1969/70 brought him more into the public focus. High-profile wins over Hibs and Rangers and an epic League Cup semi-final against Celtic, proved that he could excel against quality opposition. On 3 December 1969, he played in the Scotland team which defeated France 4-0 in an Under-23 international at Hampden. Such form and a feeling of being unsettled, meant that he was unlikely to remain at the club. In October 1970 he was sold to Sunderland where he won an FA Cup winners' medal in 1973. Further moves took him to Hartlepool United, Blackpool then Queen of the South.

	League		Scottish Cup		League Cup	
	Apps	Goals	Apps	Goals	Apps	Goals
1964/65	12	0	2	0	2	0
1965/66	36	0	3	0	8	0
1966/67	26	0	1	0	8	0
1967/68	25	7	1	0	9	2
1968/69	36	10	2	1	8	2
1969/70	33	5	1	0	10	1
1970/71	6	0	—	—	6	2
	174	22	10	1	51	7

Ian McAllister was one of four players called up from Ayr United Boys Club during the 1977 close season. He then went on to pursue an Ayr United career which has been exceeded in length by John Murphy only.

Cally's initial experience of first-team football came on 22 October 1977, when he went on as a substitute for Davy McCulloch in a Premier Division match at home to Partick Thistle. During the following month, at Molbeck, a qualifying tie in the European Youth Tournament ended Denmark 0 Scotland 2. Ian McAllister scored the two goals with his head. The second leg was won 1-0 at Somerset Park and, on that occasion, his club-mate Robert Connor played while Derek McCutcheon went on as a substitute.

In the First Division campaign of 1978/79, he was an ever-present. At this time his form at the heart of the defence was as exemplary as it was consistent. He was a worthy successor to Rikki Fleming, who had moved to Hibs in the summer of 1978. Cally displayed the composure of a veteran, thereby belying his youth. In reflection it is difficult to comprehend just why a move to a major club was not forthcoming.

The task of getting back into the Premier Division proved to be an obstinate one. Yet there were reasonable grounds for optimism at the start of 1980/81. In defeating Celtic on their own ground in the Drybrough Cup, confidence of an impending promotion push was justified. Premier League clubs Morton, Hearts and Hibs were all eliminated from the League Cup by Ayr United. Injuries and, to a lesser degree, suspension impacted on Cally's appearances in what turned into a further season of frustration for the club. In 1981/82, the promotion push again ran out of steam, but this did not reflect on the form of Ian McAllister who was named as the Supporters' Association 'Player of The Year'. The club then entered a phase of history in which First Division survival became the priority. This rendered his defensive qualities and experience to be vital assets.

On 13 April 1985, Cally scored a hat-trick of headers in a 5-1 rout of Airdrie. By that point of the season, the club had pulled clear of the relegation area but no such luxury was

afforded one year later when a descent into the Second Division took place. One point was required from the final fixture of the 1986/87 season in order to ensure an immediate return to the First Division. Heartbreak was caused by a match ending Ayr United 2 Stirling Albion 3. However Ian McAllister played the game of his life, especially during the late offensive on the Stirling Albion goal. In contrast, no such frustration was to befall the club during the next season. The Second Division Championship was won in glorious style and the trophy was presented to Cally in his role as captain. An ankle injury sustained at Arbroath had caused him to miss matches during the first half of that season and he was to be similarly unfortunate in the First Division season of 1988/89. In mid-October he was stretchered off during a rabble of a 2-2 draw at home to Dunfermline Athletic. The visitors played on and scored while he lay on the ground awaiting treatment. He was again in the situation of missing a swathe of the season with an ankle injury.

The Ian McAllister testimonial match took place on 11 December 1990, when Celtic won

2-1 at Ayr. Not that the scoreline mattered. This was also Ally MacLeod's last ever game as Ayr United manager.

Ian McAllister's last senior goal was a special one. On 28 September 1991, Ayr United trailed 3-1 with twelve minutes remaining against Morton at Cappielow Park. Greg Shaw (78 mins) and Paul McLean (82 mins) restored parity before Cally blazed a terrific drive for a stoppage-time winner. Coincidentally, his career ended in the way it had begun; by going on as a substitute against Partick Thistle at Somerset Park. The date was 14 December 1991. During the closing days of 1991, he said that he was quitting. It was a decision prompted by recurring injuries. He did play again, although in a less challenging sphere, when donning the colours of Darvel Victoria and Galston United.

Cally remains one of the greatest of the Ayr United greats.

	League		Scottish Cup		League Cup	
	Apps	Goals	Apps	Goals	Apps	Goals
1977/78	4 +5	1	0	0	0	0
1978/79	39	1	2	0	6	0
1979/80	36	3	2	0	3	0
1980/81	10	1	0	0	2	0
1981/82	38	3	1	0	6	1
1982/83	33 +1	4	1	0	5	0
1983/84	36	1	1	0	1	0
1984/85	23 +1	4	1 +1	0	2	0
1985/86	35	2	2	0	1	0
1986/87	35 +1	6	2	0	2	0
1987/88	25 +3	2	2 +1	1	1	0
1988/89	22	1	0	0	1	0
1989/90	31	2	2	0	1	0
1990/91	17 +5	3	0	0	1	0
1991/92	4 +6	2	–	–	0 +1	0
	388	36	16	1	32	1
	+22 sub. listings		+2 sub. listings		+1 sub. listing	

Alex McAnespie
Wing half, 1964-1978

'Sanny' came from Rankinston and played for Seaview Thistle, Drongan Amateurs, Cumnock Juniors and Craigmark Burntonians. Aged twenty, he signed for Ayr United during the 1964 close season. At the time he was 'a stylish wing half'. Even although he could play stylishly, supporters preferred to remember him as a hard man.

His debut came in a Second Division fixture at Dumbarton on 9 September 1964. That match was lost 2-1 but he stayed in the team against Queen of the South. These were tough times. The club flirted with extinction. Sanny became the penalty taker, so at least he had a crop of goals from the season.

In April 1966, he received a suspension which meant missing the last three League games of the season. These games comprised Arbroath away (a 1-1 draw which guaranteed promotion), Stenhousemuir away (a 4-0 win which clinched the Second Division Championship) and East Fife at home (a 2-0 win in a celebratory atmosphere).

Ayr began another Second Division quest in 1967/68. Once back in the First Division in 1969, the club's stature grew, and peaked in 1972/73. In 1973 there were trips to Canada and France. 1975 saw a return to Canada and 1976 involved tour matches in Nigeria. With

the introduction of the Premier League in 1975/76, relegation battles returned. Such battles depended on players like McAnespie.

In 1978 the club had to surrender its Premier League status and McAnespie was released. It was the end of an era.

On 8 May 1978, his testimonial took place. An Ayr United-Kilmarnock select lost 6-4 to an Old Firm select. That summer he joined Cumnock Juniors.

He managed Irvine Meadow and Stranraer.

	League		Scottish Cup		League Cup	
	Apps	Goals	Apps	Goals	Apps	Goals
1964/65	24	5	4	1	0	0
1965/66	29	2	2	0	8	2
1966/67	18 +2	0	1	0	3	0
1967/68	12 +4	0	0	0	1 +2	1
1968/69	28 +2	1	2	0	8	0
1969/70	13 +5	0	1	0	0	0
1970/71	13 +1	1	1	0	0	0
1971/72	18	0	3	0	0	0
1972/73	33	0	4	0	8	0
1973/74	31	0	4	0	5	0
1974/75	24 +5	0	0 +1	0	2	0
1975/76	23	0	3	0	6	0
1976/77	19 +1	0	1	0	0	0
1977/78	20 +1	0	0	0	4	0
	305	9	26	1	45	3
	+21 sub. listings		+1 sub. listing		+2 sub. listings	

In 1914 Neilston Victoria drew with Campbeltown Academicals, at Paisley, in the Renfrewshire Cup final. The replay was at Ayr's Beresford Park on 30 May. The Campbeltown supporters travelled by special boat for this tie. They sailed home with a 2-1 defeat to reflect on. Yet when crossing back over the Firth of Clyde, the form of Neil McBain, their eighteen-year-old inside left, must have been a topic of conversation. His display had been so good that Ayr United signed him in the Ayrshire and Galloway Hotel after the game.

He eventually made a League appearance on 20 March 1915 against Clyde at Partick Thistle's Firhill Park. The deferred date was down to involvement in active service. Hence, four years after signing, his League appearances totalled just seven. It is on record that he guested for Portsmouth and Southampton. This is consistent with the fact that he served with the Submarine Service. In addition he saw action with the Black Watch.

His Ayr United return was at home to Queen's Park on 19 October 1918, the occasion of a 2-0 win. A fortnight later, following a 5-0 demolition of Hibs, it was noted that McBain had an easy-going style. He remained a regular selection in the team despite not yet being discharged from military duty. In March 1919 it was reported that he had been discharged anyway. In February, at Hamilton, he had struck a spectacular eighty-fifth-minute equaliser in a 2-2 draw. The shot was hit with such ferocity that the ball struck the back of the net and bounced about a dozen yards back into the field of play.

A bye in the first round of the Scottish Cup meant that Ayr United did not have a first-team game on 24 January 1920. This meant that the focus was on a reserve fixture against their Partick Thistle counterparts at Beresford Park. It is not known why Neil McBain played in that match at centre half but his performance was outstanding. Yet one week later the resumption of First Division football saw him back in his normal inside left position. Common sense prevailed when he was chosen to play there in the course of a scoreless draw at home to Aberdeen on 3 April 1920. For what was left of the season the left half position was most commonly reserved for him and this situation persisted part way into season 1920/21 while also being reverted to his original inside left. Then Alex Gillespie was unavailable for a home fixture with Hibs. Neil McBain played at centre half and he was considered to be the best half-back on display. It was further observed of his centre half role that: 'That's where he has a fancy to play and where people have been wanting him to play'. Thereafter sanity prevailed, save for a few occasions when he was fielded as a winger or at wing half.

In the summer of 1921 he toured Canada as part of a Scotland squad. In November of that year he was sold to Manchester United and a further transfer took him to Everton in January 1923. While at Everton he gained two Scotland caps to add to the one he received while at Manchester United. In the summer of 1926, he joined St Johnstone. Following St Johnstone's 5-1 away win over Hibs in August 1926 much of the credit was accorded to the performance of Neil McBain at centre half. It was noted that he did little running but economised with time and energy.

In March 1928 he was transferred from St Johnstone to Liverpool and in November of that year he moved to Watford, initially as player-manager prior to becoming the manager only. In 1937/38 he was a scout for Luton Town and he was promoted to manager at that club in June 1938 after having control since March. The intervention of war temporarily halted the football career of Neil McBain and he earned a living as a joiner. In the summer of 1946 he became manager of New Brighton. On 15 March 1947, Alex Corbett, New Brighton's former Ayr United goalkeeper, had travelling difficulties in connection with a match at Hartlepool. Neil McBain deputised at the age of fifty-one years four months. The match was lost 3-0 but Neil McBain remains the oldest player to have made a Football League appearance. On 19 April 1919 he had kept goal for Ayr United on a one-off basis in a friendly at Kilmarnock yet it is still difficult to comprehend just why he volunteered himself to play in an unfamiliar position at such a mature age.

In February 1948 he became manager of Leyton Orient prior to taking up a similar position with the Argentinian club Estudiantes. During 1968/69 Estudiantes played Manchester United for the World Club Championship and some publicity was accorded to the fact that Neil McBain was the only person to have had a connection with both clubs. In April 1955 he became manager of Ayr United, leading the club to promotion in his first complete season in charge. Yet he returned to Watford as manager in August 1956, returning to take charge of Ayr United again in December 1962. He was marginally short of his sixty-eighth birthday when quitting the post in October 1963. Neil McBain remains the oldest person to have managed the club. The eighteen-year-old from Campbeltown could never have envisaged that back in 1914.

He died on 13 May 1974.

	League		Ayr Charity Cup		Victory Cup		Scottish Cup	
	Apps	Goals	Apps	Goals	Apps	Goals	Apps	Goals
1914/15	1	0	1	0	–	–	–	–
1915/16	6	2	0	0	–	–	–	–
1918/19	24	8	0	0	1	0	–	–
1919/20	35	2	1	0	–	–	3	0
1920/21	28	0	0	0	–	–	4	0
1921/22	18	0	0	0	–	–	0	0
	112	12	2	0	1	0	7	0

Andy McCall
Wing half, 1927-1935, 1940

Andy McCall joined Ayr United from Cumnock Townhead Thistle and made his first-team debut when the club was sweeping towards the Second Division Championship, in a 1-1 draw at Albion Rovers on 3 January 1928. By the season's end he had made 4 League appearances. In the First Division in 1928/29 he played in half of the League games, consolidating himself further.

His first goal was contentious. On 6 October 1928, Cowdenbeath were 1-0 up at Ayr when McCall struck. He 'palpably used his hand in scoring.' The visitors lost 3-1.

At this time he was competing for the left half position, although in 1928/29 he found himself at inside left and, to a lesser degree, outside left and left-back.

McCall became Ayr United captain. He further became an 'Honest Man' not merely through the connotations of the club's nickname. Prior to a match with St Mirren on 3 December 1932, he received a letter with a Manchester postmark. The writer offered him £50 if he would 'see to it that Ayr United lost'. He handed the letter to the board and the police investigated. Ayr United won the match 1-0 and the football writer for the Ayr Advertiser was scathing: 'There are rodents associating themselves with football who ought to be exterminated at all costs.'

McCall's stylish play was noticed by the international selectors. In November 1933 he was chosen as a reserve for the Scotland team to play Austria. Unfortunately he did not get past the fringe of selection.

Season 1934/35 was his best for scoring while with Ayr United partly due to his number of appearances as an inside forward. In November 1934, Jimmy Fleming, a centre forward, was signed from Rangers and he was made captain. The quality of McCall's performances did not dip. On 23 March 1935, with the game scoreless, he scored against Celtic, the most timely strike of his career. The final whistle was blown while the ball was being retrieved from the net.

On 28 November 1935, he joined St Johnstone for £650. In January 1939 he departed for Huddersfield Town. Then, in the summer of 1939, he went to Nottingham Forest where he played three League games prior to the war. He remained with Forest and appeared in the wartime League and friendlies until rejoining Ayr United in the closing weeks of 1939/40. Ayr United ceased playing in the summer of 1940 and he joined Clyde. By the final wartime season he was playing for Dundee, where he became a coach after gaining experience with Huntly. In October 1958 he became manager of Dundee United, resigning in April 1959.

| | League | | | Ayr Charity Cup | | Scottish Cup | |
	Apps	Goals	Apps	Goals	Apps	Goals
1927/28	4	0	0	0	0	0
1928/29	19	3	–	–	3	3
1929/30	20	2	1	1	0	0
1930/31	37	2	–	–	3	0
1931/32	38	3	2	0	2	0
1932/33	36	3	–	–	2	0
1933/34	29	2	2	0	2	0
1934/35	35	11	–	–	5	1
1935/36	11	3	1	0	–	–
1939/40	1	0	–	–	–	–
	230	29	6	1	17	4

The void League match versus Falkirk on 9 March 1935 has been included as an appearance. 1939/40: Wartime Regional League.

Walker McCall
Striker, 1976-1978

Although he was a native of Ayrshire, Ayr United signed Walker McCall from Aberdeen. That was in September 1976, when he was twenty-two. He made an immediate debut in a Premier League fixture at Motherwell. It was evident that his towering presence in the penalty area was going to be a great asset, especially since he had the heading ability to complement his physique. His headed goal at Motherwell was an accurate indication of what was to come, albeit that the match was lost 4-1.

On 6 November 1976, he headed two goals in a 2-1 win at home to Partick Thistle. In the next match he headed a further goal in a 2-2 draw away to Dundee United. His aerial threat was identifiable but difficult to counter. A strike force developed with partner Danny Masterton. The direct approach of Masterton made him menacing in the penalty area and McCall took advantage of the chances created.

In winning high balls, he often had the appearance of undergoing no great exertion. This was down to a combination of superior height and great judgement. Another facet was his ability to unleash strong drives. Nevertheless, these were fraught times. After successfully fighting against relegation in his first season, the next one brought similar pressure. Yet there were times when the pressure was relieved with some wins which were inspired by Walker McCall. 'St Mirren had their chances but Ayr had the ace card in McCall' – St Mirren 2 Ayr United 3, 2 January 1978. This was the occasion of a hat-trick which included two headers. Such results were too few to keep a part-time club in Scotland's 'Top Ten' but, in the year of writing, Walker McCall has the distinction of scoring more Premier League goals for Ayr United than any other player.

In the summer of 1978, though still an Ayr United player, he travelled to the United States to play for San Diego Sockers in the North American Soccer League. Once there he played against such luminaries as Bobby Moore, Gordon Banks, Mike England, Rodney Marsh, George Best and Alan Ball. It was a successful time and he netted fourteen goals in seventeen games.

His return from San Diego took place after the commencement of the Scottish season and he therefore missed the two opening League fixtures of 1978/79. Shortly after his return, he was offered a five-month contract to join Ajax. The offer was declined. This was soon after Motherwell had made an unsuccessful bid to purchase him. It was confidently expected that Ayr United would make an immediate return to the Premier League. That did not happen and, after a bad start, manager Alex Stuart resigned. Stuart became the manager of St Johnstone and, in November 1978, he signed Walker McCall for a second time. On the first Saturday of that month he had scored a last-minute winner in an Ayrshire derby at Kilmarnock. It was a glorious return after being out with an ankle injury. What glories might have befallen him had he accepted Ajax?

	League		Scottish Cup		League Cup	
	Apps	Goals	Apps	Goals	Apps	Goals
1976/77	32 +1	16	3	1	–	–
1977/78	34 +2	13	0	0	4	0
1978/79	10 +1	6	–	–	5	1
	76	35	3	1	9	1
	+4 sub. listings					

After signing from Parkhead Juniors, Phil McCloy was soon pressed into League action. It was the occasion of a 2-1 defeat at home to Motherwell on 5 October 1918 but it was reported that 'McCloy did very well for a first appearance'. Significantly he played at right-back against Motherwell. One week later he appeared at left-back in a 3-2 win over Hearts at Tynecastle. Thereafter it became his regular position in the Ayr United team.

Succeeding generations of supporters would be told about the full-back partnership comprising Jock Smith and Phil McCloy. Smith was acquired from Neilston Victoria in the summer of 1919 and, although a right-back at his former club, was initially selected as a winger for Ayr United. On 20 December 1919 Smith and McCloy were selected as the respective full-backs for the first time. Yet the motive was the unavailability of John Semple rather than any pretence at tactical genius. That particular match comprised a 2-1 defeat away to Raith Rovers and, one week later, Semple returned at right-back. Yet even in defeat a journalist was motivated to write: 'Philip McCloy promises to develop into one of the best full-backs in Scottish football.' The pen of the same scribe was soon being used

again to record his praise. He referred to 'the brilliancy of McCloy' while reporting on a 1-0 victory over Hearts at Tynecastle Park on 5 January 1920. In March 1920 the Smith-McCloy partnership was reinstated. Furthermore the partnership was retained but only for one more match since John Semple was the favoured right-back. Yet they were selected as the respective full-backs for the final two League fixtures of the season and this was the favoured combination from the following season onwards. The same season also saw Phil McCloy taking over as the club's penalty taker, a development caused by the departure of Switcher McLaughlan, Ayr United's original penalty king.

He became a match for the best wingers in the land. An *Ayrshire Post* report of a Scottish Cup win over Rangers in January 1923 contained three sub headings: Rangers Routed At Ayr: The Crowd Easily Accommodated: McCloy and McKenzie Great.

A midweek game at home to Falkirk in early April 1924, was by no means a key match in the history of Ayr United. Yet in later years, supporters who attended that match had a clear recollection of director Lawrence Gemson going onto the field at half-time. His mission was to inform Jock Smith and Phil McCloy that they had been chosen as the Scotland full-backs to face England in what was the first ever international match to be played at Wembley. On 12 April the big match took place with Scotland represented as follows: Harper (Hibs), Smith (Ayr United), McCloy (Ayr United), Clunas (Sunderland), Morris (Raith Rovers), McMullan (Partick Thistle), Archibald (Rangers), Cowan (Newcastle United), Harris (Newcastle United), Cunningham (Rangers), Morton (Rangers). This selection meant that three players were missing from the Ayr United v. Raith Rovers game on the same afternoon. After a 1-1 draw it was noted in the *Glasgow Herald* that: 'At the back McCloy was best, and the Scottish pair were better than Smart and Wadsworth'. In the same month his testimonial match took place. It was a low-key occasion in which Ayr United fielded three trialists in a 1-1 draw against Rangers on the evening of 28 April.

A year later Phil McCloy took part in Scotland's 2-0 win over England at Hampden. This was three weeks before Ayr United suffered relegation through failing to get the one point required for safety at Ibrox. Thereafter he played merely two matches in the Second Division. He opted to sign for Manchester City for whom he debuted at home to Cardiff City on 29 August 1925.

On 24 April 1926 he was in the Manchester City team which lost to Bolton Wanderers in the FA Cup final at Wembley. However, as in 1925, he was involved in a last-day fixture in which a draw was required to escape relegation. Unfortunately relegation was suffered in consecutive seasons when Hughie Gallacher scored a hat-trick for Newcastle United to sink Manchester City.

Matt Busby achieved legendary status in football and was even bestowed with a knighthood for his services to the game. Initially he went to England to join Manchester City and, in later years, he admitted that he seriously considered returning to Scotland due to home sickness. According to Sir Matt he was persuaded to stay by Phil McCloy. Busby was a native of Orbiston while McCloy hailed from nearby Uddingston.

In time McCloy's career wound down. He played for Chester in 1930/31 and Cork in 1931/32, although Manchester City held his registration until 1932. A subsequent move involved crossing the channel in 1933 to sign for a French club called Stade Université Rennais. It is further on record that he joined Kidderminster Harriers in January 1935.

In later life he did not forget his Ayr United connection. For example he was a spectator when Celtic visited Somerset Park for a Scottish Cup tie in February 1956. Furthermore he was a boardroom guest at that tie as was his old teammate Jimmy Hogg.

Phil McCloy passed away in 1972.

| | League | | Ayr Charity Cup | | Victory Cup | | Scottish Cup | |
	Apps	Goals	Apps	Goals	Apps	Goals	Apps	Goals
1918/19	25	0	1	0	1	0	–	–
1919/20	41	0	1	0	–	–	3	0
1920/21	39	4	1	0	–	–	5	0
1921/22	41	1	1	0	–	–	2	0
1922/23	37	2	1	0	–	–	3	0
1923/24	37	0	1	0	–	–	7	0
1924/25	26	0	0	0	–	–	0	0
1925/26	2	0	–	–	–	–	–	–
	248	7	6	0	1	0	20	0

Davy McCulloch
Midfielder, 1968-1978

Early 1969/70 remains remembered for the steady team selection and some high-profile performances. However, in terms of solidity, 1972/73 was better. Consistent results and reaching the Scottish Cup semi-finals meant that Saturdays were eagerly awaited. On the evening of 27 September 1972, McCulloch was superb in a Texaco Cup tie at Newcastle, albeit in a 2-0 defeat. However he contributed to many victories, most notably a 5-1 rout of Partick Thistle in a Scottish Cup quarter-final on 17 March 1973. He scored twice and was substituted through injury.

Season 1975/76 saw a Premier League survival battle which went to the final match. It was against Motherwell on 3 May 1976 when anything less than a win would have doomed the club. With fifteen minutes left the visitors lead 1-0. At that point the Motherwell goalkeeper dropped a cross and McCulloch touched the ball in. Five minutes later the ball appeared to be going out for a corner, but McCulloch salvaged it and played it to Gerry Phillips, who scored. Ten minutes later, time was called on a 2-1 win keeping Ayr United up. McCulloch's perseverance was the greatest factor in obtaining the result.

Ayr United signed Davy McCulloch from Kilsyth Rangers on Sunday, 31 March 1968. He was a left-sided attacking midfielder. There was an agreement that he would remain with his junior club until the season's end. Kilsyth had no game on the Saturday after his signing, so he played against Brechin City on 6 April 1968. A 0-0 draw prompted a journalist to write: 'If the Prime Minister's Cabinet reshuffle fails as miserably as Ayr United's most recent formation did... then the country is in for a rough ride.' Ayr United may have been in for 'a rough ride' in the short term but time was to be kinder.

In 1978, it was not possible to escape but he was not to play for Ayr in the First Division. He was transferred to Clydebank as part of the deal which brought Billy McColl to Ayr. A further move took him to Hamilton Accies.

	League		Scottish Cup		League Cup	
	Apps	Goals	Apps	Goals	Apps	Goals
1967/68	1	0	—	—	—	—
1968/69	32	8	2	0	8	1
1969/70	33	2	1	0	9	2
1970/71	9 +4	1	0	0	3 +2	0
1971/72	8 +1	0	0	0	2 +1	0
1972/73	30 +3	4	4	2	1 +2	0
1973/74	31 +1	2	3	4	6	1
1974/75	29 +1	5	0 +1	0	4 +1	0
1975/76	25 +10	4	2	1	2 +2	0
1976/77	29 +3	2	2 +1	0	6	1
1977/78	17 +4	2	0	0	3 +1	0
	244	30	14	7	44	5
	+27 sub. listings		+2 sub. listings		+9 sub. listings	

The history of Ayr United is littered with players who were better remembered by their nickname and here we have another fine example in the person of 'Tottie' McGhee. After failing to obtain promotion in 1957/58, manager Jacky Cox got involved in some transfer activity, albeit that wholesale changes were not required. Goalkeeper Ian Hamilton and centre half Jim McLean both debuted for Ayr United in the early part of the 1958/59 season. They had been recruited from junior football, as was Jim McGhee whose club had been Ardrossan Winton Rovers.

McGhee was thrust straight into the first team from day one, his debut being in a League Cup sectional tie at Hamilton on 9 August 1958. It ended in a 3-1 defeat but Ayr United won by the same score when the clubs met at Ayr a fortnight later. Unfortunately this phase of history saw a series of ill-tempered matches between Ayr United and Hamilton Accies and McGhee sustained an injury which kept him out for the next five games. Not even his experience of the harsh environment of Ayrshire junior football could act as an antidote against injury. After three matches back, a further injury kept him out for five matches. He returned in a 2-1 win at Dumbarton.

The first occasion of an Ayr United game being televised, was a promotion battle at home to Arbroath on 15 November 1958. In a 5-2 win, he scored in the first minute of the second half. Had the television cameras been at Somerset Park a week earlier, the footage would have included two McGhee goals in a 6-2 rout of Dundee United. At the season's end, he was able to reflect on 15 League goals and a Second Division Championship medal.

An identical number of League goals in the loftier sphere of the First Division was to bestow even greater credit on the winger with the distinctive crew cut.

Early in the 1959/60 season, a transfer bid of £15,000 from Newcastle United was declined. On 19 September 1959, the result Rangers 0 Ayr United 3 was glorious and a disproportionate share of that glory belonged to McGhee for his two first-half goals. Then, on 7 November 1959, he hit the winner in a fixture ending Celtic 2 Ayr United 3. That deciding goal was struck directly from a corner with six minutes left. In January of that year he had scored from the corner arc in a home match with Brechin City, but the goal at Celtic Park was of an eminently higher profile. He remains remembered for this above all else.

'McGhee lost much of his sparkle after being treated for a facial injury from the boot of Harold Davis' – Ayr United 2 Rangers 4, 9 January 1960. In the return League engagement with Rangers, he did manage to score again but, to put it metaphorically, his card had been marked. On Christmas Eve 1960, again at Ayr, he was once more the victim of rough treatment from Davis, although this time there was the considerable consolation that Ayr United won 1-0.

Relegation was suffered in 1961 and 'Tottie' McGhee played his last match for the club in a 4-1 home win over Stranraer on 25 April 1962. He then signed for Queen of the South. It was a short stay. In January 1963, he was signed for St Mirren by the same Jacky Cox who had plucked him from junior football in 1958. At the end of the 1962/63 season he was reinstated to junior football.

	League		Scottish Cup		League Cup	
	Apps	Goals	Apps	Goals	Apps	Goals
1958/59	27	15	2	1	5	1
1959/60	34	15	3	0	6	3
1960/61	22	2	0	0	6	1
1961/62	27	6	1	0	8	7
	110	38	6	1	25	12

On an August day in 1933 the lone figure of Terry McGibbons walked up Tryfield Place after finding it necessary to ask directions for Somerset Park. He had travelled from his native Irvine to discuss terms with Ayr United manager Alec Gibson. In 1983 he told the author that Gibson concluded the business with surprising haste. This terminated the twenty-one-year-old's link with Irvine Meadow.

McGibbons required no time to adapt to senior football. He immediately had the confidence of a veteran. By New Year in his first season he had amassed 27 First Division goals. Third Lanark in particular felt the brunt of his striking power. On the evening of 22 August 1933, Ayr United demoralised the Thirds with a devastating 7-3 result on their own Cathkin Park. He scored six! On 4 November 1933, Ayr United won 5-1 in the return League engagement and on that occasion he netted four. Ten League goals

against the same club in the same season! The praise flowed. 'He scored as good a goal as has ever been scored at Somerset Park. The ball left his foot like a rocket' – Ayr United 3 Partick Thistle 1, 21 October 1933. Match reports were consistently punctuated with such glowing references. It was a season in which Ayr United took full League points off Celtic and McGibbons scored twice in each match. This prompted Celtic's Jimmy McGrory to predict that Terry McGibbons would be a future Scotland centre forward. In April 1934 a journalist echoed a common sentiment: 'McGibbons has been one of the finest Ayr United captures in post-war seasons. His goalscoring achievements have made him a star and a much talked of player.'

As the 1934 Wembley international approached, he applied in hope for a ticket. Subsequently there was a phone call from Somerset Park to the Irvine cafe owned by his future in-laws. When his sister-in-law to be passed on the message that he would be going to Wembley he was delighted. Yet his initial assumption of a successful ticket application was incorrect. Although still inside his first senior season he had been chosen for the Scotland squad. He had to content himself with looking on while England won 3-0. McGibbons later reflected that centre forward Hughie Gallacher played well below his usual form in that match.

His goals did not bear any particular hallmark. Terry McGibbons was multi-skilled and an outstanding example of this was on 4 January 1936. In beating Albion Rovers 4-1 at Somerset Park he was the only Ayr United scorer. Two goals came from his right foot, one from his head and one from his left foot. Particularly interesting is the fact that he was adept at scoring with headers. He was not endowed with height.

Relegation in 1936 was a disappointment but the Second Division could not hold Ayr United. McGibbons was a scourge to Second Division defenders. In storming to the Championship 122 League goals were scored, 39 of which were netted by him. That overall total comprised a club record which still stands. The previous club record had been 117 League goals in 1927/28. In April 1937, Terry

McGibbons scored the record-breaking goal number 118.

During the 1938 close season, a Preston North End scout travelled to Irvine to seek him out. The Ayr United board had already declared that offers for the player would be listened to. He phoned his agreement to join Preston while on holiday in Northern Ireland.

At Deepdale there was no absence of Scots' tongues in the dressing room. Terry's new club had recently won the FA Cup with a team containing eight Scots. His deep faith made him proud to wear a shirt badge containing 'the lamb of God'. When Preston faced Arsenal at The Arsenal Stadium in the 1938 Charity Shield match, McGibbons had truly arrived at the top level. At a personal level the battle was Compton v. McGibbons. Arsenal won 2-1.

As the 1938/39 season drew to a close he became unsettled. Matters came to a head when he refused terms for the season ahead. McGibbons preferred to retrace his steps in order to play for Ayr United again. With him, from Preston, came Jacky Cox who was to become the Ayr manager in 1956.

The declaration of war meant that the First Division programme was terminated after just five games. This rendered him part time and he made no appearances in the newly convened Regional League due to the more pressing demands of work in a shipyard. It meant that he was robbed of playing at an appreciable level while still aged twenty-seven. Terry was reduced to playing for the Ayrshire Dockyard team through no fault of his own.

At the age of seventy-eight he passed away on 28 August 1990. He remains Ayr United's all-time second-highest scorer of League goals.

	League		Ayr Charity Cup		Scottish Cup	
	Apps	Goals	Apps	Goals	Apps	Goals
1933/34	38	35	1	0	2	0
1934/35	37	13	–	–	5	4
1935/36	29	11	1	2	1	2
1936/37	34	39	–	–	1	0
1937/38	35	20	1	0	5	1
1939/40	5	0	–	–	–	–
	178	118	3	2	14	7

The void League match versus Falkirk on 9 March 1935 has been included as an appearance. 1939/40: All appearances in the abandoned First Division.

Alan McInally

Striker, 1980-1984

When Alan McInally was called up from Ayr United Boys' Club in the 1980 close season, there was an air of familiarity to his surname. That was because his father, Jacky, had been a legend with Kilmarnock.

McInally came into first-team contention when he was a substitute against Clydebank on 21 February 1981. After a 4-1 win, the identical squad was named for a game at Falkirk a week later. In the second half, with the team 2-0 down, he replaced Gerry Christie. Time was called on a 2-1 defeat at Falkirk and this was followed up with a scoreless draw at Hamilton. With promotion hopes now fading, the time was right to start him. It happened on 7 March against Dunfermline Athletic. Despite outfield player Derek McCutcheon playing in goal for the entire second half, a 1-0 interval deficit was converted into a 2-1 victory. In what remained of the season, McInally was named in two more starting line-ups.

In early February 1982, Ayr United were in promotion contention prior to a winless run. However, a positive aspect was McInally's form. 'At the perfect moment he (Joe Ward) released a square pass for Alan McInally and

the youngster rifled a low first-time drive into the right-hand corner of Sproat's net' – Ayr United 1 Motherwell 1, 13 March 1982. That goal came two minutes into the second half and, in the next fixture, a midweek Ayrshire derby, he scored a marvellous goal at precisely the same time. It finished 1-1.

On 10 April 1982, McInally scored the only goal in a League fixture against Falkirk, timed at twenty-three seconds. It was the fastest recorded scoring time ever for an Ayr United goal in a competitive match. Glynn Hurst (twenty-two seconds), then Neil Tarrant (twenty seconds), eclipsed that record in later years. In the midweek, he scored two superb goals in a 4-3 defeat of Motherwell. The fans needed such performances. Growing anger was being voiced at the promotion challenge being surrendered.

The opening match of the 1982/83 season was a League Cup sectional tie, away to St Mirren. Alan McInally beat three defenders before firing past Billy Thomson. The match was lost 3-1 and a pattern set. Throughout a time of struggle, McInally shone. In 1983/84, the last League match was entered with relegation looking probable. A win was required to avoid the drop and the ensuing fixture was against Dumbarton. Dumbarton were already promoted but also stood to win the First Division Championship if a victory combined with a Morton defeat. Yet a 2-0 lead was attained. In the closing minutes, McInally tied it up at 3-0 with a solo goal.

He was the Supporters' Association 'Player of The Year' for 1983/84 and he was soon on the move to Celtic. In subsequent moves his clubs were Aston Villa, Bayern Munich and Kilmarnock. He also made 8 full appearances for Scotland and one further Ayr United appearance (for Ally MacLeod's testimonial)!

	League		Scottish Cup		League Cup	
	Apps	Goals	Apps	Goals	Apps	Goals
1980/81	3 +3	0	0	0	0	0
1981/82	15 +2	9	0	0	1	0
1982/83	32 +3	7	1	0	5	3
1983/84	33 +2	16	0	0	2	1
	83 +10 sub. listings	32	1	0	8	4

Alastair McIntyre

Alastair McIntyre was aged eighteen when he signed for Ayr United from Irvine Meadow and he was given an early debut on 23 March 1957 when Dunfermline Athletic visited. The match was won 2-1. In the midweek following his debut, he was retained for a League fixture at Airdrie. Floodlit football was still a novelty at this time therefore young McIntyre's transformation from junior football was accentuated to an even greater degree. Yet there still existed a timely reminder that senior football was not wholly glamorous. The underfoot conditions were exceptionally bad and it was noted that: 'Ayr were well and truly ground into the Airdrie mud'. That match was lost 4-1 although McIntyre's form was sound to the extent that he remained an ever-present until the end of the season.

'The man who wielded the power hammer was Alastair McIntyre – a Greenock shipyard engineer' – Ayr United 4 Morton 1, 14 September 1957. The Port Glasgow boy working in Greenock was possibly less than popular on returning to work after his contribution towards his local club's defeat. In November of that year his brother Willie also joined Ayr from junior football and history was made on 7 December when brothers appeared in the same Ayr team for the first time since the Cringan brothers had played together during the First World War.

On the Saturday preceding Christmas 1957, Alastair McIntyre found himself caught up in a game which was extraordinary even in light of the high number of goals scored and conceded in that season. It was a Second Division fixture, at Cowdenbeath, in which the home team led 4-0. Then, on the stroke of half-time, a little light was cast on Ayr United's hopes when Peter Price scored. The Ayr team then proceeded to go 5-4 ahead with four goals in the space of five minutes, culminating with two from McIntyre, the first of which he drove into the roof of the net from thirty yards. Alas, the game was lost 6-5.

In each of his first two complete seasons with the club, McIntyre managed 16 League goals. He then faced the prospect of First Division football at the outset of 1959/60 but there was a sickening development during the League Cup sectional ties which preceded the League campaign. In August 1958, in a League Cup sectional tie, a match at home against Hamilton Accies had been described as: 'More in keeping with a South American football rough house than a traditional Scottish match'. One year later, this time at Hamilton, a post-match summary stated: 'The game endorsed the feeling that bad blood has existed between the clubs. Brawn, boot and no blushes – that was the order of the day.' Jack Mowat struggled for control even although he was such an eminent official that he was destined to referee the Real Madrid v. Eintracht Frankfurt European Cup final at the season's end. Alastair McIntyre had to be stretchered off and he did not play in first-team football again until 2 January 1960 in a 3-3 draw which was contested at Motherwell. Unfortunately it was a premature return and he next played in March.

He missed the opening fixture of the 1960/61 season with a burst blood vessel. After making a return in the immediate midweek his Ayr United career remained considerably less injury prone. A return to the Second Division in 1961 was a less than alluring prospect and, on 14 December of that year, St Johnstone manager Bobby Brown purchased Alastair McIntyre for £7,000.

	League		Scottish Cup		League Cup	
	Apps	Goals	Apps	Goals	Apps	Goals
1956/57	6	0	—	—	—	—
1957/58	35	16	2	0	5	0
1958/59	36	16	2	0	8	2
1959/60	10	1	0	0	3	0
1960/61	32	9	2	1	5	0
1961/62	16	4	1	1	8	3
	135	46	7	2	29	5

Willie McIntyre
Wing half, 1957-1963

Willie McIntyre signed for Ayr United in November 1957 when he was twenty-two. He had recently been demobbed from the army and was a player with Port Glasgow Juniors at the time. His step-up from junior football meant that he was joining his younger brother Alastair at the club. Their older brother, Johnny, formerly of Irvine Meadow and Raith Rovers, was with Kirkintilloch Rob Roy at this time. This was the background to a set of brothers appearing in an Ayr United team at home to Hamilton Accies on 7 December 1957.

He was immediately farmed back to his junior club and, upon his recall, held a regular place. In the 1958/59 Championship season he and his brother played in all League fixtures. In January 1959, George McIntyre was acquired from Kirkintilloch Rob Roy and the Ayr team sometimes contained three players with the same surname, albeit that the new signing was unrelated.

Willie McIntyre was a hard man. He missed the start of the 1959/60 season through suspension then returned for a League Cup sectional tie at Hamilton. This tie resulted in his brother being put out of competitive football until beyond the turn of the season. Willie was also injured in the match and was out for two more games, both of which included missed penalties. Had he been fit, he would have taken these kicks. He had proved his proficiency during the previous season.

On 19 November 1960, an Ayr United v. Dundee game blew up after seventy-seven minutes. Ian Ure, then on the threshold of fame, was a Dundee player at the time and was back to play in his home town. Ure brought down Sam McMillan with a crude challenge. Although Ure was booked, words continued to be exchanged. Then a clash ensued between Ian Ure and Willie McIntyre. Both were sent off and what happened next was to find itself in Ure's autobiography. The book claimed that Willie McIntyre and a friend burst into the visitors' dressing room and the fists started flying again.

In January 1961, Willie McIntyre submitted a transfer request but no move was forthcoming. His steely determination was an important asset in the fight against relegation.

There was an occasion when a penalty miss had severe repercussions for Scottish football. The date was 8 April 1961. With fourteen minutes remaining, Ayr United trailed 2-1 at home to Airdrie when Alastair McIntyre was brought down for a penalty kick which Willie scored. With two minutes left, Alastair was brought down for a further penalty kick. Lawrie Leslie saved Willie's attempt but both he and Sam McMillan chased the rebound. Leslie had to be stretchered off after being caught by McMillan's boot. The England v. Scotland match was one week later and Leslie would have been in the Scotland goal, but the injury caused him to withdraw. Frank Haffey deputised and Scotland capitulated 9-3.

In this phase of history there were numerous instances of Willie McIntyre taking penalty kicks which his brother had won, but they were parted by Alastair's transfer in December 1961. Willie's last two seasons at the club were spent in the Second Division. After being released at the end of 1962/63, he went to Australia and played for Hellenic.

	League		Scottish Cup		League Cup	
	Apps	Goals	Apps	Goals	Apps	Goals
1957/58	10	0	0	0	—	—
1958/59	36	11	2	0	7	3
1959/60	30	8	3	0	2	1
1960/61	26	5	2	0	4	0
1961/62	34	5	1	0	7	1
1962/63	28	4	1	0	6	1
	164	33	9	0	26	6

Switcher McLaughlan
Wing half, 1910-1920

His real name was James but he was always referred to by his nickname. Hence, stories of 'Switcher' McLaughlan were passed on to succeeding generations. Another nickname evolved: 'The Penalty King'.

Switcher played for his local club, Kilwinning Rangers, when they won the Scottish Junior Cup in 1909. A year later he signed for the newly formed Ayr United. The inaugural League fixture was at home to Port Glasgow Athletic and, with the game scoreless, a penalty was awarded to Ayr United. At that time the captain had the right to delegate penalty kicks so Bert Tickle asked Switcher. While this was taking place, Charlie Phillips was cheekily preparing to take it himself. He missed! In the same match the club's first League goal fell to Archie Campbell, who sadly died from war wounds in 1918.

With just one competitive match played in the history of the club, a local journalist was prompted to observe that: 'Switcher McLaughlan has already established himself as a favourite'. Skill and tenacity were factors in that popularity. The fans also loved his cannonball shots. In the 1910/11 season, there was some experimentation in the penalty-taking department. A journalist noted that: 'McLaughlan's prowess as a scorer from penalty kicks is such as to inspire awe in the breast of any goalkeeper'. Switcher still holds the record for scoring the greatest number of penalties for Ayr United (see below).

In the summer of 1914 he signed a contract containing a clause compelling him to reside

permanently in Ayr but this point must have been renegotiated since he remained resident in Kilwinning. Had he complied, his Ayr United appearances would have totalled one more. In August 1915 he missed his train at Kilwinning and was unable to travel to a match at Dundee. A reshuffle was necessary and trainer Alex 'Sanny' Aitken, aged 42 years 136 days, played at outside right. Aitken remains the oldest player to have made a competitive appearance for the club. That match marked the first in the Dundee career of the great Alec Troup and the home team won 2-0.

Switcher could eliminate the threat of supposedly formidable opponents. For example it is on record that, in April 1916 he 'blotted out' no less a player than Celtic's Patsy Gallacher at Somerset Park. His importance to the team and length of service meant that he was granted a testimonial. Celtic visited on the evening of 20 August 1919. Jimmy Richardson scored twice in a 2-2 draw. The testimonial proceeds amounted to £226 18s 5d. To put it into context, this equated to almost exactly four weeks' wages for the entire playing staff at Somerset Park.

At the end of 1919/20 he was released. He went on to play for Stevenston Thistle, and then Kilwinning Eglinton before rejoining Kilwinning Rangers

	League		Scottish Qualifying Cup		Scottish Cup		Victory Cup	
	Apps	Goals	Apps	Goals	Apps	Goals	Apps	Goals
1910/11	22	4 (1)	2	1 (1)	—	— —		—
1911/12	17	8 (5)	7	0	1	0	—	—
1912/13	25	6 (2)	8	1	1	0	—	—
1913/14	31	4 (4)	1	0	—	—	—	—
1914/15	38	5 (4)	—	—	—	—	—	—
1915/16	36	5 (3)	—	—	—	—	—	—
1916/17	37	1 (1)	—	—	—	—	—	—
1917/18	32	0	—	—	—	—	—	—
1918/19	33	4 (4)	—	—	—	—	1	0
1919/20	30	3 (1)	—	—	3	1 (pen)	—	—
	301	40 (25 pens)	18	2 (1 pen)	5	1 (pen)	1	0

Brian McLaughlin
Midfielder, 1977-1979, 1986-1987

Brian McLaughlin joined Celtic from schools' football and became a full-time professional in 1971. He established himself in the first team and his form indicated that he was destined for stardom. Then his career came to a grinding halt when he suffered a cruciate ligament injury in a match against Clyde. He was sidelined on a long-term basis before fighting back into the Celtic team.

On 4 November 1977 he was transferred to Ayr United in a deal which took Joe Filippi to Celtic. There was a cash adjustment in Ayr's favour. One day later, Brian McLaughlin made his debut. With ten minutes left, and the scored poised at Ayr United 2 St Mirren 2, McLaughlin went on a run in which he evaded three defenders before lashing the ball into the net for the winner. It meant that he had endeared himself to the support after just one match.

On the last day of 1977, Celtic's visit gave him an opportunity to prove something. With two minutes left, and the score at 1-1, McLaughlin evaded two defenders and slid the ball past Latchford for the second of Ayr's Premier League wins over Celtic to that point of the season. There had been a common view that injury had robbed him of some speed and class. His earliest performances for Ayr indicated differently.

On dropping into the First Division in 1978, he just seemed to get better and better. On 16 December 1978, he scored four second-half goals in a 5-0 defeat of Montrose at Somerset Park. It was a timely boost to morale, since this match took place four days after Ally MacLeod had quit the club to manage Motherwell. McLaughlin went on to win the First Division 'Player of The Year' award. This award was backed by the Scottish Professional Footballers' Association. He also won the Supporters' Association 'Player of The Year' award. With 26 competitive goals, he was also the club's top scorer. It was a highly satisfactory season for Brian McLaughlin. The only area of imperfection was that Ayr United failed to win promotion.

In September 1979, he was sold to Motherwell, where he teamed up again with Ally MacLeod. By this time, Motherwell had descended into the First Division and this meant a relatively quick return for Brian McLaughlin to Somerset Park.

On eventually departing from Motherwell, he was sold to Hamilton Accies. His next club was Falkirk, then he played in Australia for a year. On the evening of 22 September 1986, a thirty-one-year-old trialist scored with a twenty-five-yard free-kick for Ayr United reserves. That trialist was Brian McLaughlin, who was looking for a club on his return to Scotland. He was signed again and he made a reappearance in a Second Division fixture away to Albion Rovers on the Saturday. That match, a Second Division fixture, was lost 3-2 and the season ended with the club narrowly missing promotion. He quit playing at senior level in 1987. As a coach he assisted St Mirren, Forfar Athletic, Arbroath, Montrose and Bo'ness United.

	League		Scottish Cup		League Cup	
	Apps	Goals	Apps	Goals	Apps	Goals
1977/78	22 +2	5	1	0	–	–
1978/79	38 +1	19	2	3	6	4
1979/80	5	1	–	–	2	2
1986/87	15 +13	1	2 +2	1	–	–
	80	26	5	4	8	6
	+16 sub. listings		+2 sub. listings			

George McLean
Forward, 1970-1975

George McLean was an extrovert with the footballing ability to match his character. He was initially picked up by St Mirren while playing for Drumchapel Amateurs and played for St Mirren in the 1962 Scottish Cup final. January 1963 brought a move to Rangers where he won a League Championship medal and a Scottish Cup winner's medal in 1963/64. In April 1967 he was transferred to Dundee in part exchange for Andy Penman and a further move took him to Dunfermline in March 1969. His next transfer was to Ayr United and his debut was at home to Aberdeen on 14 November 1970. In the following midweek, Newcastle lost 2-0 at Ayr in a match arranged for the official switch-on of the floodlights. McLean scored in that match then played in a 2-1 League defeat of Rangers at Ayr on the Saturday.

In February 1971, he had a cartilage operation and his appearances were further curtailed in 1971/72 due to an inability to command a regular first-team place. McLean was so frustrated that he announced a desire for a transfer in November 1971 which did not materialise. Instead he hit the best form of his Ayr United career. 'The one and only big George McLean, the man whom the fans love to hate, kept Ayr safely in the First Division by scoring four goals, two in each half. It was a real field day for the big fellow' – Ayr United 4 Dundee United 2, 15 April 1972. 'Love to hate' did not apply to Ayr United supporters. He was barracked by opposing fans.

George McLean was Ayr United's top scorer in 1972/73 despite missing ten League fixtures. In the season's opening month he was stricken with a muscle injury. On his recovery he was back to his best. On 25 November 1972, he scored the winner with a header against Dundee, but that goal became incidental in comparison to a later moment in that match. While having his shirt pulled, George McLean removed it and offered it to the offender! One week later, injury compelled him to be substituted at Perth, causing another spell out. Good times were ahead on his return. The Scottish Cup saw him in the thick of the action, especially with two goals out of the five scored at Partick Thistle in the quarter-finals.

In summer 1973 he scored 10 goals on a tour to Newfoundland. Three more followed when Ayr United followed this trip with a jaunt to Brittany. With 13 close-season goals behind him, McLean scored twice in the opening match of the season; a 2-0 win over Dumbarton in a League Cup sectional tie.

On 3 September 1973, Alex Ferguson was acquired from Falkirk. The Ferguson-McLean strike force then became known by their nicknames of Fergie and Dandy. This was not such a productive campaign and, in 1974/75, torn ligaments curtailed his appearances and goals. He was freed at the end of that season.

	League		Scottish Cup		League Cup	
	Apps	Goals	Apps	Goals	Apps	Goals
1970/71	9 +3	1	0 +1	0	—	—
1971/72	11 +9	5	1	1	0	0
1972/73	24	16	4	3	5	5
1973/74	25 +7	7	4	4	6	2
1974/75	10 +2	4	0	0	1 +1	0
	79	33	9	8	12	7
	+21 sub. listings		+1 sub. listing		+1 sub. listing	

Jim McLean

Centre half, 1958-1962

The concluding weeks of season 1957/58 saw Ayr United undergo experimentation in the centre half position. Yet the focus of Jacky Cox's attention was Jim McLean, a centre half with Baillieston Juniors. An attempt was made to play him as a trialist for an away fixture against Stenhousemuir on 15 March 1958. The response was an understandable refusal, since Baillieston still had commitments in the Scottish Junior Cup. Jacky Cox, however, was sufficiently emboldened to sign the player anyway and there was, of course, the almost standard provision that, in the circumstances, he would remain with his junior club in the meantime. Had there been no such restriction, he would almost certainly have played against an identically named player at Hamilton on 29 March 1958. The other Jim McLean was in the Hamilton Accies' forward line at this time, although he remains better remembered for his long-standing services to Dundee United.

At the outset of the 1958/59 season a journalist observed that: 'The decision of Ian Ure, blonde-haired wing half of Ayr Albion, to join Dundee comes as a disappointment to most Ayrshire fans'. Had he signed for his local club in the summer of 1958, the career development of Jim McLean may have been hindered. However he went on to display star qualities.

Jim McLean made his Ayr United debut on 16 August 1958, when Peter Price scored all of the goals in a 4-0 home win over Forfar Athletic in a League Cup sectional tie. The team was: Fulton, Paterson, Telfer, W. McIntyre, McLean, Glen, A. McIntyre, Paton, Price, McMillan, McGhee.

The Second Division Championship propelled McLean to a new level and he faced a stern test relatively early in the new season. The visit of Motherwell on 12 September 1959 meant that he would be playing in direct opposition to Ian St John, of whom great things were being said and written. St John did go on to have a fabulous career with Liverpool but he failed to score in Motherwell's 5-2 defeat at Ayr and it was noted that he was 'completely outplayed by Jim McLean'. One week later, at Ibrox, he prevented Rangers' Jimmy Millar from scoring too.

'McLean was superb at centre half, with a complete mastery of Charlie Dickson' – Dunfermline Athletic 2 Ayr United 2, 8 October 1960. Jim McLean consistently put in masterful performances at the heart of the Ayr United defence and he was rewarded with the club captaincy in December 1960. On the return to Second Division football in 1961, adverse results and dwindling crowds provided a stark and sudden transformation and it was merely a matter of time until he was plucked from this obscurity. On 17 February 1962, at Cowdenbeath, he played his last game for Ayr United. His request for a transfer was granted and he moved to Dunfermline Athletic one month after his last match. Furthermore he became club captain. In 1964/65 Dunfermline finished just one point off the top of the First Division and lost narrowly to Celtic in the Scottish Cup final. This was the peak of Jim McLean's career. Alas, his career was approaching the end. During the 1966/67 season he had to quit due to a severe knee injury.

	League		Scottish Cup		League Cup	
	Apps	Goals	Apps	Goals	Apps	Goals
1958/59	36	0	2	0	6	0
1959/60	23	0	3	0	6	0
1960/61	26	0	2	0	6	0
1961/62	25	0	1	0	8	0
	110	0	8	0	26	0

Jimmy McLeod
Centre half, 1921-1926, 1928-1933

Jimmy McLeod, a native of New Cumnock, came to the attention of Ayr United while playing at centre half for Cumnock Juniors. Following a 5-0 defeat away to Raith Rovers on 12 November 1921, Jimmy McLeod was permitted to make his debut away to Third Lanark a week later. On this occasion the margin of defeat was 2-0 but the team selection was interesting. Neil McBain had been pulled out of position to accommodate McLeod and this was McBain's last match prior to his transfer to Manchester United. McLeod remained at centre half regularly.

Throughout his career he opposed strikers of repute, such as Syd Puddefoot. On the opening Saturday of 1923, a scoreless draw was contested at Falkirk and it was on record that 'McLeod kept Puddefoot in check'. – Puddefoot went on to play for England. On 22 November 1924 Ayr United went to Falkirk in the knowledge that the home club had beaten Queen's Park 7-0 in their previous home match, Puddefoot scoring five goals. Not only did the Ayr United defence keep a clean sheet, the match was won 3-0. Alas, such successes were isolated in 1924/25 but the impending descent into the Second Division did not deter McLeod from continuing to battle for the club. After a failed promotion attempt. however, in summer 1926 Partick Thistle offered a signing but he departed to Kilmarnock on 27 August.

In summer 1928 he returned to Somerset Park, as did First Division football. During his second stint at Ayr he played the oddest match of his career. That was on 2 November

1929 and the result, a 2-0 defeat at Airdrie, is incidental. Early in the second half Jimmy McLeod was badly hurt and carried from the field. With the score at 1-0, goalkeeper Bob Hepburn was carried off. The deputy goalkeeper was McLeod! He had returned to the field. However he did have some goalkeeping experience. In Ayr United's history there are three instances of outfield players being pressed into goalkeeping action then saving a penalty. The first was at Alloa on 9 February 1926. A first-half injury to George Nisbet resulted in McLeod deputising. His save in the 1-0 win was 'magnificent'.

A match which epitomised him was the final League match of 1930/31, when a draw was needed against Kilmarnock to avoid relegation. Every player played his part in a 1-0 victory, although McLeod's appearance made him the most prominent player on the field. He played with a bandaged head!

In summer 1933 he went to Ireland to join Distillery, renewing the acquaintance of his former Ayr United teammate Jock Smith. He then joined Dalbeattie Star where Celtic visited for a first-round Scottish Cup tie in January 1934. In November 1934, Jimmy McLeod took over a tobacconist's and newsagent's business in Ayr's Alloway Street.

	League		Ayr Charity Cup		Scottish Cup	
	Apps	Goals	Apps	Goals	Apps	Goals
1921/22	20	0	1	0	2	0
1922/23	31	0	1	0	3	0
1923/24	31	0	1	0	3	0
1924/25	33	2	0	0	1	0
1925/26	30	3	1	0	0	0
1928/29	24	0	–	–	3	0
1929/30	30	2	0	0	2	0
1930/31	22	2	–	–	3	0
1931/32	35	0	2	0	2	0
1932/33	16	0	–	–	2	0
	272	9	6	0	21	0

Sam McMillan is the youngest player to have taken part in a competitive fixture for Ayr United and has the further distinction of having scored more goals for the club than anyone else apart from Peter Price.

He was born in Auchinleck and went to school there, and in Mauchline. At schoolboy level he won three international caps. Two of the matches were against England, at Wembley and Aberdeen, and the other was against Wales at Swansea. At juvenile level he represented Ballochmyle Thistle and, while connected to that club, there was a shock development. An approach was made by Ayr United manager Archie Anderson. Sam believed that he was being requested to play in a trial. In reality he was asked to play in a League fixture against Queen's Park in the daunting environs of Hampden Park. He was aged just fifteen, although he had been training at Somerset Park. In the opening minutes he suffered a bad smack in the face from the ball. It left him dazed but he played on gamely, albeit that the match was lost 2-0.

The young McMillan later played for Auchinleck Talbot then Irvine Meadow. From the latter club he joined Ayr United during the 1955 close season. In the initial match of the 1955/56 season, Charlie McNulty suffered an injury which resulted in a reshuffle for the next match. This allowed Sam McMillan to be drafted in at inside right and his form ensured that he was able to attain the status of a regular. Peter Price had also been signed that summer. The players who would become Ayr United's all-time highest scorers were in the same team. 'Without McMillan, Ayr United were like a ship without a rudder' – Ayr United 3 Albion Rovers 2, 28 January 1956. A fleeting absence, through 'flu, had a telling effect.

Promotion and relegation followed in rapid succession although there was hope for the future. Early in season 1957/58 it was noted that Ayr United had young forwards. They were Alastair McIntyre (eighteen), Sam McMillan (nineteen), Peter Price (twenty-four), Billy Fulton (nineteen) and Willie Bradley (nineteen). Goals were scored and conceded in large numbers, prompting a typical post-match observation that: 'The sparkle of the teenage forwards was dulled by the depressing display of the defence'. With key areas strengthened, the club made it back into the First Division in 1959.

'Whenever Ayr United followers reminisce on this game, they are sure to recall one second half incident... that of Ayr's Sam McMillan, about to be challenged by Stevenson, calmly – with the ball at his feet – bending down to adjust his stocking. What contempt! What cheek! What CONFIDENCE!' – Rangers 0 Ayr United 3, 19 September 1959. On 7 November that year he scored twice in Ayr United's 3-2 defeat of Celtic at Celtic Park, albeit not indulging in any mickey-taking!

On the morning of 3 May 1960, Sam McMillan arrived at Somerset Park for a training session and ended up playing against Scotland! The Scotland squad was training there in preparation for a match against Poland and Denis Law was absent. Alan

Cousin replaced Law, and McMillan played at inside left in the Young Scotland team which lost 5-1 to the full Scotland team.

After relegation in 1961, the club fell from grace spectacularly but Sam McMillan retained a loyalty which eventually ensured that he was a one-club man at senior level. His loyalty was well placed since Ayr United did rise from the depths. 'The players appeared in the directors' box and hoisted Sam McMillan on their shoulders amid a deafening roar' – Ayr United 2 East Fife 0, 27 April 1966. The occasion was the final League match of the season and the euphoria was caused by the excitement of winning the Second Division Championship under the captaincy of McMillan. Promotion had been guaranteed by drawing at Arbroath on 23 April and, by coincidence, the 4.45 p.m. winner at Sandown on that day had been called 'Super Sam'. The opening day of that month had seen his testimonial match. It was

a Friday evening match against Kilmarnock in which he scored the only goal. This also doubled up as the first leg of the Ayrshire Cup final.

His last game for Ayr United was a 1-1 draw at Dumbarton on 29 April 1968, although he remained with the club in a coaching capacity. In October 1969 he was presented with a statuette by the Scottish Players' Union. It was an award made annually to the man whom the union felt had done the most for Scottish football without being rewarded.

In November 1975 he became caretaker manager for four games following Ally MacLeod's departure to Aberdeen. New manager Alex Stuart decided, in August 1976, that he would like to bring in his own man. George Caldwell was therefore appointed in a coaching capacity and Sam McMillan's long association with Ayr United was over.

	League		Scottish Cup		League Cup	
	Apps	Goals	Apps	Goals	Apps	Goals
1952/53	1	0	—	—	—	—
1955/56	34	6	2	0	5	0
1956/57	30	4	1	0	6	0
1957/58	34	10	2	0	6	1
1958/59	36	20	2	1	7	2
1959/60	33	10	3	3	5	2
1960/61	29	6	2	0	6	1
1961/62	34	13	1	1	8	4
1962/63	33	7	1	0	6	2
1963/64	31	9	4	2	6	0
1964/65	31	1	4	0	5	1
1965/66	35	16	3	0	7	2
1966/67	27	0	0	0	7	1
1967/68	16 +1	2	0 +1	0	5	0
	404	104	25	7	79	16
	+1 sub. listing		+1 sub. listing			

In August 1945, Norrie McNeil joined Ayr United from his local club, Hurlford United. Although he had not previously been attached to a senior club, Norrie had played with and against almost all of the great players in British football at that time. On arrival at Ayr United, he had not yet been demobbed from the army and this rendered him eligible to continue playing in big representative matches. His debut was at Alloa in what was the second match of the 1945/46 season. In weather described as 'almost tropical', he lined up in this team: Corbett, Craik, Dyer, Henderson, McNeil, P. Smith, Melvin, Hunter, Malcolm, Leitch, Harper. The match was won 3-1 and the same margin of victory was recorded at home to Cowdenbeath a week later. McNeil then became temporarily unavailable for selection since he was in the Scottish Command squad for five games in Norway.

He received a similar call-up to play in an England v Scotland army international at White Hart Lane on 3 December 1945. A journalist observed that: 'Top class touches were rarer than egg and bacon breakfasts.

Only three Scots made the grade – goalkeeper Moodie (Airdrie), McNeil, Ayr United's centre half and little Deakin, the St Mirren outside left.' Another report said this of McNeil: 'Not only did he keep Lawton unusually quiet, but he also came through with the ball and used it in a way quite unusual with centre halves.' England won 3-0 and the famous Tommy Lawton scored once, but it was his only goal in three clashes with McNeil. As well as being England's centre forward, Lawton was also the First Division's top scorer in the two seasons preceding the war. Of course when appearing for the British Army, McNeil played alongside his old adversary Lawton. Also in that team was Billy Wright who was capped in 105 out of England's first 108 internationals after the war. The British Army squad played in Paris and Luxembourg under the guidance of Stanley Rous. In a game against the RAF at Stamford Bridge, McNeil, together with Sammy Cox of Rangers, conspired to close down the threat of the illustrious Stanley Matthews.

On being demobbed, there were no more external demands for Norrie McNeil but his experience was consistent with a player who really should have been playing at a higher level. Promotion from 'B' Division proved difficult to the extent that it was not achieved at all during his ten seasons at the club. This was a situation which was far from being a slight on Norrie McNeil. As expected of him, he was skilled at blotting out the potential threat of marauding forwards. In addition, he had a further dimension to his game in that he could use the ball in a constructive manner rather than be content with unceremoniously clearing the lines.

On 13 September 1950, Hibs supplied the opposition for his testimonial match. At the conclusion of that season, Hibs were to find themselves as runaway winners of 'A' Division. Despite the overwhelming quality of the opposition, the crowd saw Ayr United attain a 4-1 lead by the midway stage of the first half. Hibs rallied to draw 5-5 in a fabulous match witnessed by an attendance estimated at 8,000. Then, on 7 October 1950, Norrie McNeil became the first player to lead an Ayr

United team out for a major semi-final. The occasion was a League Cup tie against Motherwell at Ibrox. A 3-2 lead was relinquished in the closing minutes and more than half a century was to elapse before an Ayr United captain would eventually lead a team out for a major final.

'McLeod, Paton and Redpath are supposed to be in a different class from Cairns, McNeil and Nesbit, yet the Ayr trio were immeasurably superior to the visitors in every department of the game allowed by the rules' – Ayr United 2 Motherwell 2, Scottish Cup quarter-final, 10 March 1951. The replay was lost 2-1 after a goal was conceded in the final minute of extra time. McNeil, from the penalty spot, scored the Ayr goal in that tie and his performance was described as 'immense'.

Third place in 1950/51 and identically placed in 1951/52! The second place which would have brought promotion was frustratingly elusive. In October 1954, Mike Gallagher, an Eire international, was signed from Hibs and he managed to stake a stronger

Norrie in action against Motherwell in the 1950/51 League Cup semi-final.

claim to the number five shirt, albeit that a subsequent reshuffle accommodated Gallagher at wing half and George O'Donnell at centre half. McNeil was released at the end of that season. For the next sixteen years, he utilised his considerable experience in the capacity of a reserve team coach with Kilmarnock.

	League		Scottish Cup		League Cup	
	Apps	Goals	Apps	Goals	Apps	Goals
1945/46	17	1	—	—	7	0
1946/47	16	0	2	0	4	1
1947/48	30	2	1	0	6	0
1948/49	30	0	2	0	6	0
1949/50	30	1	1	0	6	0
1950/51	25	1	4	1	9	0
1951/52	29	2	1	0	4	0
1952/53	21	1	2	0	6	0
1953/54	27	0	1	0	8	0
1954/55	2	0	3	0	6	0
	227	8	17	1	62	1

Willie McStay
Left-back, 1912-1916

During Ayr United's earliest years it was possible to borrow players from Celtic at will. Willie Maley, the Celtic manager, was a friend of Lawrence Gemson, an Ayr United director. Furthermore Charles Maley, Willie's eldest brother, was a popular priest in Ayr and a regular in the directors' box at Somerset Park. These links enabled Ayr United to benefit from being able to borrow players from Celtic. Sometimes it would be a short-term arrangement running to one match. In other instances, as with Willie McStay, the arrangement would periodically be renegotiated until running for several years.

Willie McStay was born on 21 April 1894 in Netherburn. His football career began with Netherburn Juniors, prior to a move to nearby Larkhall Thistle. In 1912 he joined Celtic and, in November 1912, came to Ayr United on loan. On the last day of that month, he made his debut in a 0-0 draw at Dunfermline.

By the end of McStay's first season, Ayr United had retained the Second Division Championship and, by dint of successful lobbying by club chairman Tom Steen, the club gained the requisite number of votes for promotion. For the challenge ahead, Willie McStay was installed as club captain, even though still at the tender age of nineteen. By coincidence 1913/14 got underway at Celtic Park, which would prove to be the scene of many future glories for McStay. These were to be Celtic glories as was this one in 1913. Ayr United lost 5-1 but gradually acclimatised to the more testing nature of First Division football. With David Thomson now at Airdrie, Willie McStay's full-back partner was now John Bell. It was a partnership which endured until McStay's eventual recall.

On 25 September 1914, Willie McStay got married. One day later he appeared for Ayr United in a home match with St Mirren. It is on record that: 'McStay had to run the gauntlet of a shower of confetti as he emerged from the pavilion to take part in the match'. Despite that match being lost, Ayr United sat in a creditable fifth position in the completed League table of 1914/15, beaten for fourth place by Morton having a better goal average. One year later that fourth place was attained and it remains the highest League finish ever by an Ayr United team. Such consistency under McStay's captaincy would undoubtedly have been well noted by the club holding his registration. Consequently he was recalled by Celtic during the 1916 close season.

During what remained of the First World War he had spells guesting for Belfast Celtic and Distillery. He then remained with Celtic until 1929, by which time he had won League Championship medals in 1917, 1919, 1922 and 1926. The medal haul was supplemented by him playing in the Celtic Scottish Cup-winning teams of 1923, 1925 and 1927. He was further honoured with 13 appearances for Scotland. On departing Celtic, he played for Hearts during 1929/30 prior to an appointment as manager of Glentoran.

Willie McStay was a great uncle of Paul McStay who also achieved fame with Celtic and Scotland. Another of his great nephews was Jock McStay, whom Ayr signed in 1996.

Willie McStay retained an affinity for Ayr. Prior to playing a League Cup sectional tie at Kilmarnock on 30 August 1950, the Ayr players had a telegram wishing them success from 'The two backs of 1914'. The senders were John Bell and Willie McStay.

| | League | | Scottish Cup | | Ayr Charity Cup | |
	Apps	Goals	Apps	Goals	Apps	Goals
1912/13	17	0	1	0	2	0
1913/14	38	0	Club did not qualify		0	0
1914/15	37	0	—	—	1	0
1915/16	34	0	—	—	1	0
	126	0	1	0	4	0

Billy Middleton

Outside right, 1913-1920

In the summer of 1913, the Ayr United directors had to address the issue of recruiting players who could help the club maintain a challenge in the loftier sphere of the First Division. One of those players was Billy Middleton. He was from County Durham but was signed from Brighton & Hove Albion.

In October 1913 it all began to fall into place, as he scored a coat-trick in a 4-0 win over Motherwell. A coat-trick? Each autumn from 1910 until 1913 a local tailor operated an incentive. An overcoat was awarded to any Ayr United player scoring twice in a home League match. A further coat would go to a spectator nominated by the player.

The international situation meant that it was just a matter of time before he would exchange his position in the Ayr United front line for a considerably more dangerous front line. In 1915 he signed up for the Ayrshire Yeomanry, thereby curtailing his season, although not his football. For instance in March 1916, in an army match at Aldershot, he formed a right-wing partnership with Joe Cassidy, a former Ayr United teammate.

Middleton reappeared for Ayr United at the outset of 1916/17. The third League match of the season was a visit from Celtic. The difficulty was compounded by the non-appearance of Middleton and goalkeeper Gordon Kerr. In consequence Ayr United began the game with ten men, including John Bell, a full-back, in goal. Celtic scored in the third minute. Bell was relieved of his duties by the arrival of Middleton who kept a clean goal

in a 1-0 defeat. In December 1916 Middleton 'departed for somewhere at the seat of war'. That 'somewhere' was France. Terrible form caused the following to be written in February 1917: 'The team's decadence dates from about the time Billy Middleton went abroad.'

He returned to play for Ayr United in September 1917. In March 1918 his name again disappeared from the team but his return to France was brief. By the next month he was out of the fighting again due to a shot left hand. No more emergency goalkeeping!

In 1918/19 a 'vast improvement' was attributed to 'the return of Richardson and Middleton from France', albeit that Middleton still missed the occasional match. At the conclusion of 1919/20 he was sold to Aberdeen for £250. Former club Brighton & Hove Albion received £90 and the player received £50 while Ayr United banked £110. Further moves took this fine Ayr United captain to Southend United and Dumbarton. He then returned home to County Durham.

In 1938 Middleton was appointed North of England scout for Luton Town. The Luton Town manager at the time was Neil McBain, his former Ayr United teammate.

| | League | | Scottish Q'fying Cup | | Ayr Charity Cup | | Victory Cup | |
	Apps	Goals	Apps	Goals	Apps	Goals	Apps	Goals
1913/14	31	5	1	0	1	0	–	–
1914/15	32	5	–	–	0	0	–	–
1915/16	16	0	–	–	0	0	–	–
1916/17	15	4	–	–	–	–	–	–
1917/18	23	8	–	–	0	0	–	–
1918/19	27	5	–	–	1	0	1	0
1919/20	22	4	–	–	0	0	–	–
	166	31	1	0	2	0	1	0

Scottish Cup: In 1913/14 Ayr United did not qualify. The competition was then suspended up to, and including, 1918/19. Billy Middleton did not make a Scottish Cup appearance in 1919/20 therefore the competition has been excluded from the tabulation.

Dougie Mitchell
Midfielder, 1966-1974

Dougie Mitchell was capped for Scotland Schoolboys Under-15 in 1964. He played against Wales, Northern Ireland and England. The England game was at Dens Park and a reporter wrote 'Mitchell was tremendous'. Don Revie was in attendance and signed Mitchell for Leeds United's youth team. However, he failed to settle and returned to Ayr before 1964/65 had expired.

His next club was Crosshill Thistle. At this time good young players trained at Somerset Park. When Dougie turned up under this arrangement, manager Tom McCreath denied him training facilities because his hair was too long! That was in March 1966 but, by the start of the following season, the club relented and he made his debut in a League Cup sectional tie against Cowdenbeath.

On 25 February 1967, Ayr United v. Motherwell was postponed and rescheduled for the following Wednesday. This meant that Dougie had to withdraw from the Scotland Youth squad. For Ayr United he scored two goals in a 3-3 draw with Motherwell.

He exuded style and authority, especially upon the club's return to the First Division in 1969. Then, in January 1971, in response to a transfer request, the club agreed that he could depart at the right price. No move took place.

At the outset of season 1973/74, he was out of the starting line-up but was selected for a comeback at Dunfermline on 13 October 1973. The result was Dunfermline Athletic 0 Ayr United 4. On 19 January 1974 victory over Hibs would have put the club into joint-third place with Rangers, but a 1-1 draw was still enough to remain in fourth place. On the last weekend of January, a 5-0 Scottish Cup win at Cowdenbeath included a Dougie Mitchell goal. The season ended with a 1-0 win at East Fife and Mitchell scored.

At the start of 1974/75 he was still playing well. In a League Cup sectional tie on 14 August, he scored with a penalty in a 3-2 win over Celtic. He was now in the twilight of his Ayr career. In November 1974, Johnny Gibson was acquired from Partick Thistle. As part of the deal, Mitchell and Doug Somner moved the other way. Further moves took him to Queen of the South and Whitletts Victoria. An injury suffered against Darvel compelled him to quit playing at twenty-nine. As youth coach, he returned to the Ayr staff.

	League		Scottish Cup		League Cup	
	Apps	Goals	Apps	Goals	Apps	Goals
1966/67	24 +2	2	1	0	4 +1	0
1967/68	28 +4	5	1	0	9 +1	0
1968/69	33 +1	6	2	0	7	0
1969/70	34	1	1	0	10	0
1970/71	27	2	1	0	4	0
1971/72	12 +2	2	0 +2	0	6	0
1972/73	8 +6	0	0 +2	0	0 +3	0
1973/74	23 +2	2	4	1	0 +3	0
1974/75	1 +4	0	–	–	5	2
	190	20	10	1	45	2
	+21 sub. listings		+4 sub. listings		+8 sub. listings	

Eddie Monan
Centre half, 1964-1968

In 1960, Eddie Monan won a runners-up medal after playing for Ramblos Amateurs against Minishant in the 1960 Scottish Amateur Cup final. He moved on to Ardeer Recreation then Irvine Meadow before joining Ayr United at the age of twenty in the summer of 1964. On 8 August 1964, in a League Cup sectional tie at Berwick, he was one of seven players making an Ayr United debut. There was a common view that he was the best player afield, albeit in a 3-1 defeat. 'The defence stood solid around big Eddie Monan and gave Morton's much-praised attack a lean time' – Ayr United 0 Morton 1, 12 August 1964. The tall, lanky defender was also impressive on his home debut.

He developed into a centre half in the Jacky Charlton mode in that he liked to press forward to lend his height to the attack at set pieces. This was especially true in 1965/66 during the successful pursuit of the Second Division Championship. He was cool to the point of arrogance. This point is borne out by the fact that he would occasionally stoop down on one knee while heading clear.

First Division football in 1966/67 did not afford the same opportunities to entertain the crowd. From 17 December 1966 until 11 February 1967 (inclusive), Ayr United lost ten consecutive League matches. In the midst of that was a Scottish Cup defeat at Elgin, setting the club record for consecutive defeats at eleven. The last game before that run was a 0-0 draw against Clyde at Shawfield, an excellent result against the team which would finish third in the table. Eddie Monan played in the Clyde fixture but an ankle injury prevented him from playing during the dire spell. In fact he only made the starting line-up in one of the eleven losses in that sequence and that was the final one, at home to a Celtic side on course for winning that season's European Cup. His presence at the heart of the defence had been badly missed.

One League victory was recorded by Ayr United that season. It came on 8 April 1967 when the result Ayr United 1 St Johnstone 0 brought relief that the club had evaded the ignominy of completing the campaign without a League win. A post-match summary gave forth the opinion that: 'The win stemmed from a solid half-back line in which Eddie Monan was an outstanding centre half. He never put a foot wrong.' Quite apart from his defensive input, he made another contribution, scoring the decisive penalty kick.

During 1967/68, Shrewsbury Town bid £6,000 for the purchase of Monan. The offer was declined. In light of subsequent events it would have been better if the offer had been accepted. During the 1968 close season, the club secretary was ill and had to be admitted to hospital. Before suffering his illness, the registration forms had been prepared in readiness for sending off to the Scottish Football Association. Eddie Monan's form was inadvertently omitted. By virtue of a clerical error, he was a free agent. He then opted to sign for Partick Thistle on a free-transfer basis.

In 1997, while in Canada, he died of stomach cancer.

	League		Scottish Cup		League Cup	
	Apps	Goals	Apps	Goals	Apps	Goals
1964/65	26	0	2	0	5	0
1965/66	33	1	3	0	8	1
1966/67	22 +1	2	0	0	7	0
1967/68	24 +3	2	0	0	9	2
	105	5	5	0	29	3
	+4 sub. listings					

Eddie Moore

Centre forward, 1964-1967

Eddie Moore looks on while Billy Muir loses out to the Partick Thistle goalkeeper.

Eddie Moore joined Ayr United from Beith Juniors at a bad time when attendances had diminished dramatically. Against that sombre background, Moore made his debut away to Stenhousemuir on 28 March 1964. He scored a well-taken goal in a 2-1 win. His home debut saw an attendance which was less modest than normal. This had nothing to do with beating Stenhousemuir but everything to do with the fact that Scotland v. England tickets were being sold inside the ground. A game ending 1-4 to Hamilton Accies was almost incidental. Moore was the Ayr scorer and this was illustrative of a developing pattern – Moore was becoming an ace marksman in a struggling team.

On 22 August 1964, Moore and Drew Nelson scored a hat-trick each in a 6-0 rout at home to Berwick Rangers in a League Cup sectional tie. All of Moore's goals were headers. The Berwick result was unrepresentative of Ayr United's form at this time. Yet Moore continued his goalscoring ways regardless. On 12 September 1964 he scored another hat-trick of headers in a Second Division fixture at Dumfries, although Queen of the South won 4-3. It was a result which left the club with no League points from the five matches played.

November of that year brought news that the Ayr United board were considering selling Somerset Park to pay off debts. Within several days, this news prompted three clubs to make an offer for Moore. The story was broken by the *Sunday Express* in an article accompanied by a photograph of almost-deserted Somerset Park terraces on the day before. Yet the match played on that day comprised a 2-1 win over Montrose in which Moore scored the two Ayr goals.

'Ayr United must not sell Moore, unless, of course, someone bids in the region of £20,000' – Ayr United 3 Stenhousemuir 0, 12 December 1964. Another isolated win and another Moore hat-trick! It was followed by three defeats then a 3-1 win over Queen of the South on 2 January 1965. Moore scored with two headers in that match to take his total to five headed goals in the two League matches between the clubs that season. The final 1964/65 Second Division table confirmed a second-from-bottom finish but Moore could reflect on a season in which he netted 32 competitive goals.

A successful push was made for the Second Division Championship in 1965/66 and it is odd to relate that the Ayr United career of Moore went into decline. His goalscoring ratio was comparable to that of 1964/65 but he found himself selected for only half of the thirty-six League fixtures. The arrival of Alex Ingram in the summer of 1966 hastened the end of Moore's time at the club and he submitted a transfer request in January 1967.

Ayr United's opening League fixture of the 1967/68 season was at home to Clydebank, whom Moore had recently joined. Four minutes into the match he scored but the result was a 3-1 Ayr win.

	League		Scottish Cup		League Cup	
	Apps	Goals	Apps	Goals	Apps	Goals
1963/64	5	4	–	–	–	–
1964/65	33	23	4	4	5	5
1965/66	18	13	2	0	5	2
1966/67	11	2	0	0	0	0
	67	42	6	4	10	7

Eric Morris

Utility player, 1979-1985

On the evening of 11 September 1979, spectators at Ayr United *v.* Dunfermline Athletic spotted two new players in the home line-up. These players were Eric Morris and David Armour, both signed from Rangers. Adverse results caused the attendance to be only 1,668, but the stay-at-homes must have regretted missing a 3-0 win in which Morris scored in the fourth minute of his debut. Eric Morris joined as a striker. By the end of his Somerset Park career, he had the reputation of the ultimate utility man.

Eric Morris originally played for Muirkirk Juniors. A move to Troon Juniors took place and, in a further transfer, he went to Irvine Meadow where he won a Scottish Junior Cup winner's medal in 1973. He was named Scottish Junior Football's 'Player of The Year' for 1972/73 and joined Rangers. While there, he played in every position, albeit that his goalkeeping stint was in a five-a-side tournament. At Ayr too, he played in a variety of positions.

He was selected to play for the Scottish League against the League of Ireland. The venue was Dublin's Dalymount Park on, fittingly, St Patrick's Day, 1980. The match was lost 2-1, but it recognised his form. That summer, Scotland won a four-nation semi-professional tournament in Holland. In a 4-2 win over England, the Scotland goals were scored by Ayr United players; Robert Connor (2), Eric Morris and Gerry Christie.

The first competitive match of 1980/81 was a Drybrough Cup tie with Celtic. It was frustrating and two Ayr goals were disallowed. Justice was done when Morris headed the only goal. The participating clubs were the four highest-scorers from the previous season's Premier Division and the top two from both the First and Second Divisions. A disproportionate number of Premier Division clubs meant that the competition was geared towards a crowd-pulling final. During the Paisley Fair, a St Mirren *v.* Aberdeen final took place at Hampden Park. The crowd figure was disappointing and the competition scrapped.

Injury caused him to miss the start of the 1982/83 season. This was a campaign in which he was to play in a variety of positions, although mainly as sweeper. He was voted the Supporters' Association 'Player of The Year'.

In 1983/84, his appearances were restricted by achilles tendon trouble. This put him into the 'long-term injury' category. At the start of 1984/85, he made a welcome return to the Ayr defence. This was his last complete season at the club. In November 1985 he said that he was quitting due to work commitments. He later played for Cumnock Juniors and Craigmark Burntonians and rejoined Ayr United as a youth coach.

	League		Scottish Cup		League Cup	
	Apps	Goals	Apps	Goals	Apps	Goals
1979/80	34	11	2	0	2	0
1980/81	36	10	1	0	10	4
1981/82	35 +2	8	1	0	6	0
1982/83	26 +2	0	1	0	0	0
1983/84	18	0	1	0	0	0
1984/85	30 +2	1	2	1	2	0
1985/86	1 +2	0	—	—	0	0
	180	30	8	1	20	4
	+8 sub. listings					

Malky Morrison

Centre forward, 1945-1950

Malky Morrison's early career took him from Third Lanark to East Stirling to Cambuslang Rangers. In 1945 he was in the Cambuslang Rangers team which beat Burnbank Athletic in the Scottish Junior Cup final. Burnbank then successfully lodged a protest and, when the final was replayed, the outcome was reversed. The protest was at the inclusion of Morrison who was still registered with East Stirling. Soon afterwards he signed for Ayr United.

His debut was in a 4-1 home win over Dumbarton on 8 September 1945. It was a scoring debut. The goals then flowed consistently. On the first Saturday in October a daunting trip to Dundee was faced. To that point of the season the home team had dropped just one League point. The result was a 4-1 victory to Ayr and Malky scored a hat-trick. One week later he scored four in a 6-0 victory away to Stenhousemuir. The return League engagement, on 5 January 1946, was won 10-1 and he scored six on that day. Ten League goals against the same club in the same season! It was reminiscent of Terry McGibbons against Third Lanark in 1933/34.

He was a sergeant in the Highland Light Infantry and was conveniently stationed at Glasgow's Maryhill Barracks, prior to being demobbed in February 1946. Despite his goalscoring, there were times when he found himself playing for Ayr United reserves in the South of Scotland League. On 11 October 1947 the reserves beat Whithorn 15-1 at Somerset Park. Malky scored six, including a hat-trick in marginally over two minutes. This was in spite of missing most of the second half with an ankle injury. Yet even although he was in and out of favour, he is in the list of Ayr United's top ten scorers of all time.

Morrison loved scoring. Following a 4-2 win over Dunfermline on 21 February 1948, it was written: 'There have been complaints in recent days of a lack of personalities in Scottish football – men who amuse the crowd, and whose cantrips and little characteristics are recognised and eagerly awaited both by home and away spectators. If this is so, then Ayr United are singularly fortunate in possessing one well established favourite.' He also had a ruthless streak. After a 0-0 draw with Hamilton Accies a week later, Norwood, the visiting goalkeeper, refused to shake hands with Malky because he had laid him out cold in a collision. Harassing goalkeepers was one of his traits.

'Malky Morrison reproduced all his old pep and slit the opposing defence ragged as of yore' – Arbroath 1 Ayr United 1, 2 October 1948. Unfortunately his 'old pep' was of little avail when he tore a ligament in the penultimate League fixture that season, a fortnight after he had netted four in an 8-0 win over Dundee United.

Morton's visit for a League Cup sectional tie marked the opening of 1949/50. Malky's opener was badly received by Jimmy Cowan, the goalkeeper. Cowan hounded the referee all the way to the centre of the field because the ball had been punched into the net. In formal tones one journalist wrote: 'His fist was the agent of propulsion'. Perhaps justice prevailed as Morton won 4-3.

His final game was at Hamilton on 18 February 1950 and he was freed at the end of the season. His next club was Newton Stewart of the South of Scotland League.

	League		Scottish Cup		League Cup	
	Apps	Goals	Apps	Goals	Apps	Goals
1945/46	22	29	—	—	7	6
1946/47	11	4	0	0	4	3
1947/48	19	15	1	1	5	5
1948/49	21	18	0	0	6	5
1949/50	4	1	1	0	6	6
	77	67	2	1	28	25

John Murphy
Left-back, 1963-1978

John Murphy holds the club record for the greatest number of competitive appearances and also for the longest Ayr United career span. He began with Saxone Amateurs, Hurlford United then Darvel Juniors before signing for Ayr United in July 1963. He became known by the nickname 'Spud'. His debut came on 10 August 1963 with a visit from Morton in a League Cup sectional tie. The match was lost 1-0 and it was a reasonable result given that Morton were on the brink of an all-conquering season.

The final match of his first season was won by a solitary goal... a 'Spud' Murphy goal! In a midweek win over Dumbarton, he scored from forty yards. He was never noted for scoring but his career would bring him a goals total which crept into double figures.

The momentum of the club's struggle carried over into 1964/65 then, almost miraculously, there was a transformation. With full-back partner Dick Malone playing on the right there was stability and a rapid ascent to the First Division took place in 1966. Too rapid! From 1967/68, John Murphy was club captain. This was at a time when a push was being made to regain a First Division place. It took until 1969 to accomplish this.

Now consolidated in the First Division, 1970/71 opened without Murphy, who injured a knee. It was a temporary setback. For this and the next two seasons, he was to be an ever-present in Ayr United's League fixtures. However when Malone joined Sunderland in October 1970 the Malone-Murphy partnership was broken up.

Ever-reliable throughout the early seventies, it was made known in the summer of 1974 that 'Spud' was in line for a testimonial which took place on the evening of 12 March 1975, when Danish club Aarhus were beaten 4-1. In order to qualify for the impending Premier League, it was necessary to finish in the top ten in the First Division table of 1974/75. Seventh place was attained.

He was released at the end of 1977/78, by which time Robert Connor had laid claim to the number three shirt. John Murphy played for no other senior club. However he did do scouting work for Aberdeen at the request of Alex Ferguson, a former teammate.

	League		Scottish Cup		League Cup	
	Apps	Goals	Apps	Goals	Apps	Goals
1963/64	33	1	3	0	6	0
1964/65	36	1	4	0	6	0
1965/66	27	0	2	0	8	1
1966/67	34	1	1	0	8	0
1967/68	36	0	1	0	10	0
1968/69	34	2	2	0	7	0
1969/70	32	0	1	0	10	1
1970/71	34	0	1	0	1	0
1971/72	34	0	3	0	6	0
1972/73	34	1	4	0	8	0
1973/74	27 +1	1	4	0	6	0
1974/75	34	0	2	0	2	0
1975/76	35	1	3	0	6	0
1976/77	24 +1	0	1	0	6	0
1977/78	5	0	1	0	1	0
	459	8	33	0	91	2
	+2 sub. listings					

Craig Nelson

Goalkeeper, 1998-2003

During 1997/98, Ayr United were served by two very good goalkeepers. They were David Castilla and Kristjan Finnbogason. When the latter returned to Iceland, there was a glaring need for goalkeeping cover. It transpired that Craig Nelson was to bring a lot more than cover.

His early career had involved playing for Airdrie, Partick Thistle, Hearts and Falkirk, from whom he moved to Ayr at the age of twenty-seven. He signed on 13 July 1998, the day before flying to Sweden for a club tour. At the start of the season proper, Castilla was retained in goal. Then, on 5 September 1998, he had a bad game in a 3-2 defeat by Hamilton Accies. The next match was a visit from Rangers in a League Cup quarter-final tie. Craig Nelson was selected and showed great composure, albeit that the tie was lost 2-0. It was the start of a run of appearances.

There was some experimentation involving Thomas Gill, Jens Knudsen and Marius Rovde in 1999/00, but Nelson ranked well above them all for consistency. A particular strength was his ability to win one-on-one situations; the type of situation in which a goalkeeper would not be remotely faulted for losing a goal. Penalty kicks could be similarly viewed and Nelson distinguished himself with his part in a shootout in a Scottish Cup replay against Dundee on 15 February 2000, saving kicks from Gavin Rae and Nicky Banger.

'Craig Nelson made an outstanding save to thwart the dangerous Curran' – Ayr United 1 Morton 1, 18 November 2000. Reports were regularly punctuated with similar references. By 2001/02, Nelson had seen off all competition for the jersey. On 9 October 2001, another of those shootout situations took place at Somerset Park. Even extra time had failed to produce a goal for Ayr United or Kilmarnock in a CIS Cup tie. Kick number ten fell to Killie's Craig Dargo, who would have put his team through by scoring. Craig Nelson saved it and, two kicks later, Ayr United won the tie. Further progression in the competition took the club to the now famous Hampden semi-final against Hibs. It was necessary to repel Hibs' attacks during extra time in addition to regulation time. The last line of the Ayr defence was patrolled by Craig Nelson. In the closing seconds (literally) he clutched a strong shot to his chest. That save rendered the tie as good as won.

In the 2002 CIS Cup final against Rangers, he again flourished at Hampden. Six minutes in, he saved a Lovenkrands shot from point-blank range. Given the size of the occasion, it was vital to repel Rangers in the early part of the match. It was Nelson's second major final as a First Division player. He had played for Falkirk in the 1997 Scottish Cup final.

He came through a phase when there was a large turnover of players at Somerset Park. Craig Nelson proved himself a good club man and a better goalkeeper.

During the 2003 close season he signed for St Johnstone and in August 2004 he went to Brechin City on loan.

	League Apps	Scottish Cup Apps	League Cup Apps
1998/99	15	0 +3	1
1999/00	18	4	1
2000/01	26 +8	0 +1	1
2001/02	35	5	5
2002/03	31	2	1
	125 +8 sub. listings	11 +4 sub. listings	9

Andy Nesbit
Left half, 1946-1954

Andy Nesbit was signed from Kello Rovers on 21 March 1946 and his debut came nine days later when drafted in for a League Cup match with Stenhousemuir. Although inexperienced at this level, Nesbit was aged twenty-four at the time and he fitted in comfortably in a 2-2 draw. Nesbit's debut was the final match of a section which ended in a dead heat between Ayr United and Dundee United. In the ensuing midweek, a playoff match was won 1-0 by Ayr United at Hampden. That tie brought forth the following press comment: 'The Ayr club could hardly improve on the present middle line – Smith, McNeil, Nisbet (*sic*). The last named lived up to the standards of those who saw him against Stenhousemuir and, with experience, should blossom into a really first class player.' It was a glowing tribute from a journalist who got the name wrong. He was not alone. In the early part of his senior career, Andy Nesbit was persistently referred to as 'Nisbet'.

On his arrival at Ayr, the League fixtures had already been completed. This was the first season of the League Cup competition and it was as an end-of-season competition in this inaugural campaign only. Having disposed of Dundee United, Nesbit then played in a quarter-final tie which was lost 2-0 in front of an 18,128 attendance at Dundee's Dens Park.

The remit of a left half in the forties was not diverse. It was a job which entailed containing the threat of the opponent playing in the inside right channel and distributing the ball sensibly. To Andy Nesbit it further involved scoring the occasional goal. This may all sound very simplistic. In reality it was

tough. Andy Nesbit stood at no more than 5' 8" but could hold his own against ostensibly more intimidating adversaries. He became the team's penalty taker while developing a liking for taking free-kicks.

Throughout his time at Ayr, the club played in 'B' Division although there was a glimpse of glory in October 1950 when a League Cup semi-final was contested against Motherwell at Ibrox. That tie was unluckily lost 4-3. Nesbit had to go off injured for more than twenty minutes, during which time Motherwell equalised the early Ayr opener. It was noted that: 'When Nesbit came back on, he was a passenger on the wing, but when the teams reappeared for the second half, Hugh Good (trainer) appeared to have used some form of magic, for Nesbit was back in his old position with barely a trace of a limp. As we were to see later in the half, Andy Nesbit's return was as gallant a display of fortitude against physical pain as anyone could wish to see.'

On the evening of 19 September 1951, his testimonial match ended Ayr United 2 Queen of the South 3. Such occasions should really be something of a stroll for the player being honoured. In this match it was so different and he found himself putting in a hard shift. Yet the testimonial did not mark the end of his Ayr United career. Andy Nesbit was not released until the end of season 1953/54.

	League		Scottish Cup		League Cup	
	Apps	Goals	Apps	Goals	Apps	Goals
1945/46	–	–	–	–	3	0
1946/47	25	7	2	0	4	0
1947/48	29	3	1	0	6	1
1948/49	23	3	2	0	6	2
1949/50	28	3	1	0	6	1
1950/51	26	2	4	0	6	0
1951/52	29	2	1	0	6	0
1952/53	16	0	0	0	4	0
1953/54	14	0	1	0	0	0
	190	20	12	0	41	4

In the summer of 1979, Stevie Nicol was one of three players called up from Ayr United Boys Club. It was the start of a career which was to see him propelled to the heights of being one of the great players of British football. His first-team debut was in a First Division fixture at home to Arbroath on 20 October 1979. The team was: Rennie, McColl, Kelly, McSherry, Nicol, Fleeting, Frye, Armour, Morris, Connor, Christie. Substitutes: Masterton, Lindsay. Although destined to be a great left-back, he played as a central defender in that initial appearance. The opportunity had been afforded by an injury to Ian McAllister in a car accident. Nicol's good performance was not the main talking point. Post-match conversation mainly related to Arbroath having two players dismissed in Ayr's 2-1 win.

For the next match, McAllister regained his place. Then, during the next month, regular left-back Willie Kelly announced that work pressure was going to prevent him from continuing to play. As a consequence, Robert Connor was reverted to left-back from the midfield position in which he had been playing. On 5 January 1980, Stevie Nicol appeared in the starting line-up at left-back for the first time. The result, Ayr United 4 Hamilton Accies 1, meant that the team had undergone sixteen consecutive League games without defeat. The club record of seventeen had been set in 1958/59 and, alas, it was to remain the club record. It was an incidental statistic in comparison to the future of Stevie Nicol. From that date onwards he became Ayr United's regular left-back.

Nicol immediately displayed the attributes expected of a good full-back. He was strong and decisive in the tackle and had good passing skill. Beyond this he displayed further skills which would normally be considered to be outwith the role of a defender. To suggest that he was good on the overlap would be tantamount to understating his ability to surge upfield. He could ghost past opponents with consummate ease thereby getting into attacking situations. Stamina was not an issue. Stevie Nicol was able to revert from defence to attack and back again in a manner which had the illusion of being effortless.

In the opening League fixture of 1980/81, Motherwell lost 5-0 at Ayr. Stevie Nicol was as polished as ever, although this game was largely remembered for his goal from a diving header. Transfer speculation gathered momentum and it was generally accepted that the Scottish First Division could not contain such a footballing talent indefinitely. When 1980/81 gave way to 1981/82, the club remained in the First Division. On the Tuesday evening of 20 October 1981, he played against Denmark in an Under-21 international. The following day he was sold to Liverpool for £300,000 after a meeting between the respective managers, Willie McLean and Bob Paisley. It was the highest transfer fee ever received by Ayr United and the amount was not eclipsed until the deal involving Gary Teale two decades later.

At Liverpool, he won Football League Championship medals in 1984, 1986, 1988 and 1990. His medal haul further included being an FA Cup winner in 1986, 1989 and 1992. He won twenty-seven full Scotland caps, fourteen Under-21 caps and had the distinction of being named 'Football Writers' Player of The Year' for 1989. Nicol was in the

Liverpool team which won the European Cup in 1984 and he also appeared in the ill-fated final at the Heysel Stadium one year later. His Liverpool career extended from October 1981 until February 1995 and he even ascended to the club captaincy.

After terminating his long association at Anfield his clubs, in turn, were Notts County, Sheffield Wednesday, West Bromwich Albion (on loan), Hull City and Doncaster Rovers. At Notts County he had been a player-coach under the managership of Howard Kendall. On moving to the United

States, he was able fully to realise his coaching potential, initially with Boston Bulldogs and then with New England Revolution. He won the 2002 MLS 'Coach of The Year' award for taking New England Revolution from the bottom of the Eastern Conference to the top.

In the programme for the first home match after his Ayr United debut, the following was written: 'Stevie Nicol was the red-headed stranger in the first team on Saturday, for those of you who did not recognise him.' His period of being unrecognised was decidedly temporary!

Stevie Nicol hails a delighted crowd after scoring against Motherwell.

	League		Scottish Cup		League Cup	
	Apps	Goals	Apps	Goals	Apps	Goals
1979/80	18 +2	2	2	0	0	0
1980/81	39	3	1	0	10	0
1981/82	11	2	–	–	6	1
	68	7	3	0	16	1
	+2 sub. listings					

George Nisbet

Goalkeeper, 1917-1926

AYR'S NISBET.

George Nisbet moved from Petershill to Ayr United during austere times. The First World War continued to exact its toll while the people at home had to contend with rationing and the threat of bad news from France. Nisbet's debut in the Ayr United goal on 3 February 1917 was therefore a low news priority. This argument is compounded by the fact that Dundee, then second-bottom of the League, won 2-1 and the game was described as 'about the poorest exhibition of football ever taken part in by the Ayr United team'. Blame was not accorded to Nisbet. He showed sufficient confidence to be retained for the next match, a 1-0 away defeat against Rangers. 'Nisbet is the right man for the Ayr goal' was a press comment following his next match, a 1-1 draw at home to Clyde.

Active service was beckoning for Nisbet. He played in the first three League games of 1917/18 prior to being called-up. In keeping with national security it was not reported where Nisbet was posted to but the course of the war at that time indicates that it was probably Flanders. The following season saw him guard the Ayr goal just twice (while on leave).

He reappeared in October 1919 and close scrutiny of match reports is indicative that Nisbet was fearless. Injuries caused him to complete fewer matches than he started. In time his courage would terminate his Ayr United career. Yet his bravery seldom caused him to be unavailable and in the three seasons from 1920/21 until 1922/23, he was in the starting line-up for every competitive match. The run of consecutive appearances was halted when Nisbet was rested for a League fixture at Easter Road on 2 February 1924.

In November 1923, a social evening was held in his honour. Lawrence Gemson, the club chairman, presided and a 'handsome timepiece' was presented. He had been honoured by the club at an earlier date. His testimonial was on 30 August 1922 despite his Ayr United career span not being especially long to that date. Celtic provided the opposition for a match drawn 2-2.

In May 1924, John Hughes, the Celtic reserve goalkeeper, was signed by Ayr United and at the start of 1924/25 was selected ahead of George Nisbet. After appearing in the first thirteen League fixtures, Hughes was deposed by Nisbet who returned for a home match against Dundee which was won 1-0. It is on record that 'he got a great cheer when taking the field'. But the season brought little in the way of cheer. In a classic example of a team not living up to the sum of its parts, relegation was suffered and when the club re-emerged three years later the goalkeeper was no longer Nisbet. At a fixture at Alloa on 9 February 1926 he suffered a head injury. Not only did he take no further part in the game, he took no further part in any Ayr United game.

	League Apps	Ayr Charity Cup Apps	Scottish Cup Apps
1916/17	12	–	–
1917/18	3	–	–
1918/19	2	0	–
1919/20	15	1	0
1920/21	42	1	5
1921/22	42	1	2
1922/23	38	1	3
1923/24	36	1	7
1924/25	20	1	2
1925/26	28	0	1
	238	6	20

Jim Nisbet
Outside right, 1926-1931

Jim Nisbet was destined to emulate his cousin Johnny Crosbie, who had become an international while at Ayr United. Both were from Glenbuck.

Nisbet was signed from Cumnock Juniors and his Ayr United debut came in a Second Division fixture against Stenhousemuir on 30 October 1926. The 1-1 result was the club's seventh League draw of the season and Nisbet was not selected for the first team again until 5 February 1927. From then on, he was a regular. His goals included two in a 4-2 win over St Bernard's in Edinburgh.

The following season the Second Division Championship was won in a goalscoring frenzy. Nisbet was on the right wing and Tommy Kilpatrick the left, while inside forwards Danny Tolland and Billy Brae further supplied the chances which Jimmy Smith converted. Nisbet did not lack success himself. On 24 September 1927, he scored a hat-trick in a 7-0 win over Forfar Athletic.

In May 1928, the club journeyed to Scandinavia for a tour. The first match was won 2-1 against Gjoa. Nisbet was a scorer. For the next game, two days later, the team endured a train journey to Stockholm of thirteen-and-a-half hours. Nisbet again scored, the match ending Sweden 1 Ayr United 3. The tour was completed with three more matches back in Norway. By coincidence, he found himself playing in Norway a year later. He was chosen to go on the SFA's continental tour, the first match being a 7-3 win over Norway in Bergen. Nisbet had the distinction of scoring twice in that match. Two days later he again scored. This time it was a 4-0 win over an Oslo select. The date of that match was 28 May 1929. One of the games he had played for Ayr United in that same city had been on 27 May 1928. Déjà vu must have prevailed. The Scotland tour was concluded with a 1-1 draw against Germany in Berlin and a 2-0 win over Holland in Amsterdam. These were deemed unofficial matches but were subsequently conferred with full international status. That was the background to Nisbet's 3 appearances for Scotland. Although playing in all four matches, the one against an Oslo select did not comprise an international. Jim Nisbet remains the player with the most Scotland appearances while with Ayr United.

In October 1930, having made 6 League appearances, Nisbet's name disappeared from the team when he was replaced by Ernie Suggett. From that point he made just one more first-team appearance. That was in a Scottish Cup tie at Bo'ness on 14 February 1931. The tie was summarised thus: 'The thirty or thereby supporters who followed Ayr United to the shores of the Firth of Forth, bade a tearless farewell to the team's existence in this season's Scottish Cup competition.' It was a stark contrast to the earlier part of a career which had involved a Second Division Championship win, foreign tours in consecutive years and 3 international caps.

He was freed in the same month as the Bo'ness tie. Former Ayr United player Neil McBain spoke to him in his capacity of Watford manager. The author was unable to find a record of him signing for Watford, but it can be categorically stated that he played for Nithsdale Wanderers in May 1931.

| | League | | Ayr Charity Cup | | Scottish Cup | |
	Apps	Goals	Apps	Goals	Apps	Goals
1926/27	14	4	1	0	0	0
1927/28	37	13	1	0	2	1
1928/29	36	6	–	–	3	1
1929/30	36	7	2	1	2	1
1930/31	6	0	–	–	1	0
	129	30	4	1	8	3

Arthur Paterson

Outside left, 1964-1967

Arthur Paterson originally stayed in Glasgow, but the family moved north and his career began with Inverurie Locos. His first senior club was Aberdeen and he then played Army football while on national service. He later played for Irvine Meadow where he had the distinction of being in a Scottish Junior Cup winning team. On the Friday evening of 8 May 1964, 1,569 people turned up at Somerset Park to witness Craigmark Burntonians defeat Irvine Meadow 4-3 in the Western League Cup final. Two players on view were on the brink of signing for Ayr United. Arthur Paterson, then aged twenty-four, was one of them. The other one was Craigmark's Alex McAnespie.

Paterson's flamboyant wing play made him popular with the fans. His close control, electrifying bursts and long-range drives were all facets of his play. 'Arthur Paterson beat three defenders, took a rebound from another defender and brought goalkeeper Andy Crawford to his knees with a shot from close range' – Ayr United 2 Dumbarton 1, 15 August 1964. The sequel to that run was that Bert Whittington easily scored after the ball had been fisted out in his direction. This was in the first minute of Whittington's debut. In future years he was to become a professor.

As the season progressed, Paterson was tried at centre forward for a run of games, even although his skills were clearly associated with those of a winger. In time he was permitted to drift back to his true position. 'Arthur Paterson smashed the ball into the roof of the net from thirty yards' – Ayr United 5 Brechin City 1, 13 March, 1965. This was a description of one of his two goals on that afternoon.

From the beginning of 1965/66, the team had fresh impetus and Arthur Paterson revelled in the transformation. The season opened with a 5-2 home win over Stenhousemuir in a League Cup sectional tie and Paterson's goal was typically classy. It was described as 'an amazing solo effort'. Another dimension to his play was an ability to take dangerously inswinging corners. His corner technique was even compared to that of former Ayr United winger Alec Beattie.

His runs were devastating and he had the knack of being able to beat an opponent in a small space. Sometimes all of the facets of his play would combine to spectacular effect. For example, at Somerset Park in December 1965, he beat two East Stirling defenders then scored from the edge of the penalty area. It was a goal with the Arthur Paterson hallmark stamped on it. 'Arthur Paterson beat three Airdrie defenders in an amazingly short space before crashing a left-foot shot past McKenzie' – Ayr United 1 Airdrie 1, 12 March 1966. With both teams vying for the Second Division Championship, this was a vital strike.

Entering the First Division as champions of the Second Division, hopes that 1966/67 would be a season of consolidation were soon dispelled. It was a season of supreme struggle. Arthur Paterson thrived on attacking football. His style and natural skills depended upon it. Illustrative of the situation was the fact that no player scored more than four League goals for the club in that season. As an attacking force, the team was impotent. Through no fault of his own, Paterson did not have the opportunities to flourish.

Of the players released at the end of that season, Arthur Paterson was one of three to join Clydebank. The others were Eddie Moore and Harry Rutherford.

	League		Scottish Cup		League Cup	
	Apps	Goals	Apps	Goals	Apps	Goals
1964/65	27	5	4	2	4	0
1965/66	35	12	3	2	8	5
1966/67	10 +11	0	1	0	4 +3	1
	72	17	8	4	16	6
	+11 sub. listings				+3 sub. listings	

The year is 1988 and George Watson is receiving a trophy from Peter Price (second left). Completing the photograph are Stevie Evans (second right) and Bill McWilliam of Ayr United Travel Club.

Peter Price remains the most prolific Ayr United goalscorer of all time and his influence was such that his time at the club could accurately be described as 'The Price Era'. His career began with Craigmark Burntonians and he then progressed to St Mirren after turning down the opportunity to play in a second trial match for Celtic reserves. After being released by St Mirren, his next club was Gloucester City. While there, he played in a floodlit friendly in which Gloucester beat Spurs 2-1. At the age of twenty-three, he returned to his native Ayrshire and was signed by Neil McBain for Ayr United in the summer of 1955. The transfer was from Gloucester, although conflicting reports that he joined from Darlington were not wholly inaccurate. His registered club had given him permission to guest for Darlington owing to an army posting to that area.

The return to his Ayrshire roots soon developed into a story of goalscoring abandon. For example he netted five in an 8-1 rout at home to East Stirling on 26 November 1955. Such form was far from isolated. In winning promotion 103 League goals were amassed and Peter Price had the honour, at Forfar, of getting the milestone 100th. The same goal comprised his fortieth League strike of the season.

A sojourn into the First Division proved all to brief. This was to prove a bad development for Second Division defences. In the two seasons 1957/58 and 1958/59, he scored 105 competitive goals. On 29 March 1958, Ayr United trailed 4-1 in a League fixture at Hamilton. Quite remarkably Price scored four in eight minutes to win the match 5-4. The goal times were seventy-two, seventy-three, seventy-eight and eighty minutes. No one would have dared to write such a story in fiction. It was harsh that such prolific scoring should have gone unrewarded in terms of the club's promotion quest. There was no such frustration in the Championship season which followed. 'This was one of Price's best ever games. He matched his legendary goalscoring act with slick and intelligent ball play' – Ayr United 3 Morton 0, 6 September 1958; 'Every time Price got the ball, City's defence panicked' – Brechin City 0 Ayr United 4, 18 October 1958; 'You could almost see the worry on the faces of the Alloa defenders when Price was in possession near goal' – Ayr United 6 Alloa Athletic 2, 25 October 1958. Yet he was more than a penalty-box finisher. In the course of a 3-0 Scottish Cup win, at home to Stranraer, he started a run at the halfway line, which culminated in him beating all challenges to get through on goal and net a shot which was described as 'unsaveable'. It was considered to be: 'A goal that will be talked about at Somerset Park for many a day'.

Once back in the First Division, his menace was still greatly in evidence. On 12 September 1959 a highly rated Motherwell team lost 5-2 at Ayr and the occasion was marked by a Price hat-trick. Reputations did not matter to him. On 23 January 1960, television crews from BBC and STV descended on Somerset Park for the visit of a Hearts team which was destined to win that season's First Division Championship. After a 1-1 draw, one journalist described what he considered to be 'one of the wildest displays of jubilant supporters in a decade'. While 1-0 down, a Bobby Thomson clearance fell to Sam McMillan who broke clear before picking out Peter Price. The ace predator met the ball on the run and advanced on the Hearts goal before beating Gordon Marshall with a left-foot shot. It was a goal which put the fans into a feverish mood of excitement due to the timing of it. It was the last development of the game. There was not even sufficient time left to re-centre the ball.

The fickle nature of football was illustrated in October 1960 when Jacky Cox dropped Price for a game at Dunfermline. He was the club's top goalscorer to that point of the season. Nevertheless he found himself playing reserve football and he remained out of contention for four matches at this stage. On returning there were signs that the magic was still there. On Christmas Eve 1960 he got the only goal in a win over Rangers and he was headline news again. Disappointingly the season ended in relegation and he refused terms in the summer of 1961.

The 'Price Era' ended on 4 January 1962 when he signed for Raith Rovers. Prior to the end of the 1962/63 season he was an Albion Rovers player, although not for long. In April 1963 he emigrated to Australia where he played for Gladesville. On his debut for that club he scored a hat-trick against Hakoah with less than half an hour played. It is a fact that his first touch of the ball in Australian football resulted in a goal. The goals continued to flow but he was unhappy there and flew home amid a threat of being reported to FIFA for breach of contract. It was a hollow threat since, in June 1963, the Australians were still negotiating for entry to FIFA.

To reflect on the Ayr United career of Peter Price is to reflect on a goalscoring phenomenon. He is one of eight players to have scored at least 100 competitive goals for the club... and he is the only one to have broken through the double-century barrier. A true Ayr United great!

| | League | | Scottish Cup | | League Cup | |
	Apps	Goals	Apps	Goals	Apps	Goals
1955/56	35	40	2	1	5	0
1956/57	32	21	1	0	6	4
1957/58	34	46	2	1	6	7
1958/59	35	37	2	2	8	12
1959/60	32	17	3	5	6	4
1960/61	19	5	0	0	6	3
1961/62	12	7	1	0	4	1
	199	173	11	9	41	31

Stan Quinn

Centre half, 1966-1973

Stan Quinn was an uncompromising centre half, a stopper in the true sense. Despite this, he was not tall. He was signed from Shettleston Juniors in the summer of 1966 and, for the first competitive match of the new season, he made a piece of history. This was the first season in which substitutes were permitted in Scotland, and Quinn was Ayr United's first 'twelfth man'. The occasion was a League Cup sectional tie at Berwick on 13 August 1966. On that afternoon he was not called upon but, in the midweek following, he made it into the starting line-up as a deputy for the injured Eddie Monan. That was at home to Raith Rovers, again in the League Cup, and it was scoreless. A further sectional tie brought Cowdenbeath to Ayr on the Saturday and Stan Quinn made another piece of history by being the first Ayr United player to go on as a substitute in a competitive match at Somerset Park. This happened when he replaced Sam McMillan.

At this stage of history, Quinn only wore the number five shirt when Eddie Monan was unavailable. Yet at other times he lined up, in the number four shirt, alongside Monan. His position was scarcely relevant. He did not waver from his role as a stopper.

During the 1967/68 season, Manfred Mann entered the UK charts with his rendition of *Mighty Quinn*. With typical opportunism the terracing songsters of Somerset Park made up a slightly altered version: '*Come on without, come on within, you've not seen nothing like the Stanley Quinn*'. At the end of that season, the club lost Eddie Monan due to a clerical misdemeanour. This left Ayr's 'Mighty Quinn' as the key man in defence.

On 2 August 1969, a friendly took place which ended Ayr United 1 Bolton Wanderers 2. It was not a remarkable match. However, in retrospect, the starting line-up is interesting. It was the first time the following team was selected: Stewart, Malone, Murphy, Fleming, Quinn, Mitchell, Young, Ferguson, Ingram, McCulloch, Rough. In the months ahead, the fans knew that this would be the regular selection, save for suspension and injury. Stan Quinn was captain of that team. The 1969 League Cup semi-final, together with the replay, comprised two epic ties against Celtic. Stan Quinn failed to retain all of his teeth and it became a part of local folklore that the dislodged ones became embedded beneath the Hampden turf.

At the end of 1971/72, he was awarded the Ayr United Supporters' Association 'Player of The Year' trophy. In his acceptance speech, he mentioned that he preferred to leave the ball play 'to those endowed with greater skills'. Yet Stan Quinn was selling himself a little short. He was capable of being more constructive than he gave himself credit for.

In July 1973 he was transferred to St Mirren and, in January 1974, decided to quit playing.

	League		Scottish Cup		League Cup	
	Apps	Goals	Apps	Goals	Apps	Goals
1966/67	22 +1	0	1	0	3 +2	0
1967/68	25 +2	0	1	0	5 +3	0
1968/69	35	0	2	0	8	0
1969/70	24 +1	0	0	0	10	0
1970/71	24	0	0	0	6	0
1971/72	21	0	2	0	5	0
1972/73	3	0	0	0	8	0
	154	0	6	0	45	0
	+4 sub. listings				+5 sub. listings	

Centre forward, 1914-1921; manager 1923-1924

In season 1912/13 Sunderland won the Football League Championship and contested the FA Cup final. That final, at Crystal Palace, was lost 1-0 to Aston Villa. On that afternoon at Crystal Palace, Jimmy Richardson played in front of a crowd of 120,081. By the time the following season had expired he was an Ayr United player. Initially he had joined Third Lanark from Kirkintilloch Rob Roy, before going to Sunderland in 1910. His success in England was inconsistent with a move to Ayr United. Where was the logic in it? The answer was revealed to the author in a conversation with a grandson of Jimmy Richardson. He stated that his grandmother had been unable to settle in Sunderland. It was most fortunate that Ayr United had the opportunity of signing a quality striker due to the player's wife missing Scotland.

On 14 March 1914 he made his debut at home to Kilmarnock. That game was scoreless but Richardson was soon on the goal trail. Several days later, on the Tuesday, Clyde were beaten 2-1 at Shawfield and he scored both Ayr United goals. Even this early in his Ayr United career, Richardson's quality was glaring to the extent that there was press speculation about the terms of his transfer from Sunderland. Why the speculation? An enquiry directed at the player would have clarified that his acceptance of terms was principally motivated by Somerset Park being located in the west of Scotland. The season finished with him averaging a goal per game from the nine League fixtures played for the club.

In season 1914/15 the centre forwards for the first team and the reserves both had the surname Richardson. Yet there was no confusion whatsoever. For example after a game at Hamilton, early in the season, it was observed that: 'Richardson was in a class by himself'. There was only one Jimmy Richardson and the goals flowed consistently. In October 1914 a second-half hat-trick brought about a 4-0 win over Hibs at Easter Road. The fact that Ayr United had won 5-0 at the same venue in January of that year hardly mattered. Richardson's performance was witnessed by a large number of khaki-uniformed troops of the Ayrshire Yeomanry, then based at Cupar. A week later, during the course of a 1-0 home win over Celtic, an injury to goalkeeper Lyall caused Richardson to take up temporary goalkeeping duties. Fortunately it was a brief spell of duty during which he had nothing to do.

The question as to whether football should continue, became the subject of scathing debate. International matches and Scottish Cup ties were suspended while the League continued in the fraught circumstances caused by the war. At the end of season 1914/15 Richardson had 29 League goals to his credit. It was the largest seasonal haul by an Ayr United player to that time.

A fourth placed League finish in 1915/16 remains a club record and it was a season in which Hearts in particular felt the brunt of Richardson's marksmanship. He scored a hat-trick in a 5-0 rout at Tynecastle and repeated the feat in a 3-1 win in the return match at Somerset Park. Hearts were placed second in the League when losing the latter mentioned fixture in January. Richardson was on the brink of military service. During the course of the next two seasons he made one solitary League appearance while on leave. He had been located to 'somewhere in France'. Football League Championship and an FA

Cup final appearance to trench warfare in three years!

On returning from France he was hospitalised with stomach trouble. Against that background little was expected on the occasion of his Ayr United comeback. The occasion was a home match versus Hibs on 2 November 1918. Quite remarkably he scored a hat-trick in a 5-0 win, thereby prompting a headline of 'Richardson's Rampant Return'.

On 22 February 1919 he played in the second half only in a League International against England at Birmingham (yes, a substitution in 1919). Then, on 5 April, he played the whole match in the return at Ibrox and he succeeded in scoring twice in a 3-2 win over the Football League. Jimmy Richardson therefore became the first player to gain a representative honour while attached to Ayr United. Also in April 1919 he played for the full Scotland team against Ireland at Windsor Park and England at Goodison Park.

On 4 January 1921 he was granted a testimonial in which Ayr United drew 3-3 with a League Select. The match yielded £112 at the gate in addition to the value of tickets which had previously been sold. Yet his last game for the club was approaching. That match was on 5 March 1921 at Kilmarnock. His Ayr United career had began against the same club seven years earlier. A transfer request was lodged and, in time for the 1921/22 season, he signed for Millwall after persistent efforts from Bob Hunter, their manager.

At the start of 1923/24 he returned to Ayr United as manager. A year later he took over at Cowdenbeath and 1924/25 became what remains the best season in that club's history, finishing fifth in the League, just two points behind Celtic. In subsequent managerial spells he was at Third Lanark and Falkirk.

Jimmy Richardson was spotted at Somerset Park for a Scottish Cup quarter-final tie against Motherwell on 10 March 1951. On 31 August, in the same year, he died in Glasgow.

| | League | | Ayr Charity Cup | | Scottish Cup | | Victory Cup | |
	Apps	Goals	Apps	Goals	Apps	Goals	Apps	Goals
1913/14	9	9	1	1	—	—	—	—
1914/15	37	29	1	1	—	—	—	—
1915/16	34	25	—	—	—	—	—	—
1917/18	1	0	—	—	—	—	—	—
1918/19	20	16	1	2	—	—	1	0
1919/20	34	22	1	0	3	1	—	—
1920/21	24	8	0	0	2	0	—	—
	159	109	4	4	5	1	1	0

He remains the club's third highest scorer of League goals despite missing more than two seasons due to active service.

Jacky Robertson
Inside forward, 1952-1955

Jacky Robertson came from Aberdeen and he played for the local Stoneywood Juveniles. He progressed to Huntly where he attained the captaincy. At the age of twenty-three, he then joined Ayr United in January 1952, in which month he made his debut in a 4-0 win at home to Forfar Athletic. It was a scoring debut with his goal coming in the final minute.

'Robertson has the tireless energy to keep a defence continually on the stretch. Thanks Mr Anderson (manager) for bringing more than a glimmer of hope to a somewhat jaded spectatorate' – Ayr United 3 Falkirk 1, 12 January 1952. This was only his second match for the club and again he was a scorer.

Jacky Robertson's nickname was 'Danny Kaye' in view of his close resemblance to the American comedy star. However it was not a Hollywood lifestyle for Jacky. On moving to Ayr, a job was found for him as a butcher.

In 1953, the Scottish Cup second-round draw gave Ayr a trip to Buckie Thistle. Fans of Huntly took the opportunity of travelling the relatively short distance with the express purpose of seeing Jacky Robertson. That was the background to the cheers he received on scoring both of his goals in a 5-1 win.

Owing to a cartilage operation he did not make an appearance in 1953/54 until Boxing Day. As on his debut, he struck with a last-minute goal. This time the margin of victory was 3-0 and the opponents were Arbroath.

Even in adversity his appetite for the game was undiminished. At this stage he was close to fulfilling his wish to play at centre forward. That wish materialised on the evening of 1 September 1954 when he scored twice in a 4-2 win at Brechin in a League Cup sectional tie. He was retained at centre forward for a prolonged spell in which one of the earlier matches saw him achieve a hat-trick in the opening League fixture (Albion Rovers 4 Ayr United 5). In that season he missed just one League fixture. That one fixture was a 9-0 defeat away to Third Lanark!

On 1 August 1955, Jacky Robertson was sold to Portsmouth where he made his debut against Charlton Athletic. A particular experience was playing against the 'Busby Babes' at Old Trafford on 2 April 1956. Another match involved a 4-2 defeat by Manchester City, in which he scored twice against the legendary Bert Trautmann.

Season 1957/58 was spent with York City. Then, in the 1958 close season, he went to Canada to play for a Toronto club called Polish White Eagles. It was a short stay. He came back across the Atlantic and played for Barrow for the four seasons from 1958/59 until 1961/62 (inclusive). At Barrow he played in an FA Cup tie against Wolves who were the reigning Football League Champions. The outcome was Barrow 2 Wolves 4 and he scored the two home goals despite being in direct opposition to Billy Wright.

For season 1962/63 he joined East Stirling. It proved to be a promotion-winning season but Jacky's last game for them was on 3 November 1962. On the following Saturday he was due to give his sister away at her wedding. The club, however, insisted that he had to play in an away fixture against East Fife. Family loyalty came first. His contract was immediately terminated.

In later years he lived, worked and retired in Prestwick, becoming an occasional spectator at Somerset Park, while retaining an affinity for his hometown club, Aberdeen.

	League		Scottish Cup		League Cup	
	Apps	Goals	Apps	Goals	Apps	Goals
1951/52	11	3	1	0	–	–
1952/53	25	14	1	2	6	3
1953/54	7	2	0	0	0	0
1954/55	29	19	5	5	7	5
	72	38	7	7	13	8

Tommy Robertson

Right-back, outside right, 1929-1934, 1939-1940

His native locality and his speed caused Tommy Robertson to be known as 'The Patna Flyer'. Approximately half of his Ayr United career was spent as a right-back, although he was better remembered for his performances from the time he was switched to the wing.

After a pre-season public trial match on 1 August 1929, he agreed to sign for Ayr United. His previous club was Tongue Row and he was described as 'a well built youth of 5ft 9ins'. His uncle, Jack Robertson, had been a full-back with Rangers and Southampton.

Tommy Robertson's debut took place at Somerset Park on 19 October 1929 when Dundee United were crushed 6-1. Thereafter Robertson remained a regular at right-back.

Illustrative of his speed was the fact that he was a Powderhall sprinter. The decision was made to use his pace at outside right and his first competitive outing in his new position was at Airdrie on 27 February 1932. En route to that match he was standing on a station platform when a train came in. Someone opened a door before the train had stopped, resulting in the door slamming into Tommy Robertson's back. He suffered concussion and, after a rest, played. In a 2-2 draw he did well.

Robertson did not score at Airdrie but he found the net in each of the next three matches. One of those goals came in a 5-0 rout of Cowdenbeath at Ayr and was described as 'spectacular', as he had to evade three opponents.

Season 1932/33 should have been one of great opportunity. He was facing the first complete campaign since the discovery of the position most suited to him. Alas, he was facing a time blighted by injury. On

3 September 1932, injury compelled him to leave the field during a League fixture against Hearts at Tynecastle Park. He returned but suffered a further spell of absence later in the season. On returning again he was spectacular. That was against Dundee at Somerset Park on 8 April 1933 when scouts from Arsenal and Newcastle United were in attendance. In a resounding 6-0 result, Robertson scored four.

In February 1934 his name disappeared from the team and he was only recalled once more for first-team duty prior to a transfer to Dundee on 18 July that year. His four-goal performance had obviously been well remembered by the Dundee board. On 15 October 1936 he moved to Clyde whom he represented in the 1939 Scottish Cup final in which they defeated Motherwell 4-0.

'The Patna Flyer' again donned an Ayr United shirt between November 1939 and February 1940 in the Wartime Regional League. During this phase of his career it was reported that he was 'engaged in work of national importance'. Ultimately a knee injury ended his second spell at the club. His manager at Ayr in that wartime season was Frank Thompson who became boss at Glentoran during 1945/46. Tommy Robertson joined him as a player there.

| | League | | Ayr Charity Cup | | Scottish Cup | |
	Apps	Goals	Apps	Goals	Apps	Goals
1929/30	24	1	1	0	2	0
1930/31	13	2	–	–	0	0
1931/32	35	11	1	0	2	1
1932/33	13	8	–	–	3	1
1933/34	26	7	0	0	1	1
1939/40	14	5	–	–	–	–
	125	34	2	0	8	3

1939/40: Wartime Regional League.

His real name was Charlie Rodger but from his boyhood days he was 'Fally'. This mention of his younger days is an appropriate introduction to his career. The Mackie Cup was a coveted trophy in Ayr Schools football and it was won first by Newton Park School in June 1923. Fally played at outside left, scoring two penalties for the victorious team.

In his youth he played three games per week. He played in both the Shopkeepers League and the Workshops' League before turning out for the juvenile Craigview Athletic on Saturdays. While with Craigview Athletic he had a brilliant match in a juvenile cup final at Somerset Park on the last Saturday in June 1931. He was signed by Ayr United inside a fortnight.

Rodger's first-team debut was on Boxing Day 1931, a 3-1 win at Hamilton. By the season's end he had made two more League appearances and one in the Scottish Cup, all at left half. Yet when he became a regular it was at outside left. At the outset of 1932/33 that position was held by Pearson Ferguson and it was later occupied by Billy Brae. Ferguson was loaned to Queen of the South to assist them in their promotion push and, from February, Fally Rodger played on the wing.

On 30 September 1933 an Ayr United v. Kilmarnock match was preceded by much ceremony due to the grand opening of the covered enclosure at the railway end. Fally Rodger's equaliser in a 1-1 draw was described thus: 'Rodger outpaced his challengers but seemed to be at too acute an angle. He shot and the keeper never saw the ball until it was in the net. Many fans behind the goal claimed they did not see the ball leave Rodger's foot. It was one of the best goals seen in the history of the Ayrshire county derbies'.

In 1934/35, Ayr United flirted dangerously with relegation. Crucially, the penultimate League fixture was won 3-2 at Motherwell. Rodger got the decisive goal. A week later, despite defeat at Airdrie, the escape was completed as St Mirren failed to win their final game. This brought a wave of relief, although relegation was deferred by only one year. By then, however, Fally Rodger was no longer an Ayr United player. On Wednesday, 30 October 1935, he played for the Scottish League against the Football League at Ibrox. This recognition was doubtless instrumental in a move to Manchester City, whom he signed for on Monday 2 December 1935.

March 1938 saw him move to Northampton Town. He was released in summer 1939 and rejoined Ayr United in November of that year. On 13 January 1940 an emergency required him to play in goal for an entire match. He saved a penalty and the result was Celtic 1 Ayr United 3.

In June 1940 Ayr United closed down for the war but, prior to being called up for military service in 1943, he played for Partick Thistle and Dumbarton.

	League		Ayr Charity Cup		Scottish Cup	
	Apps	Goals	Apps	Goals	Apps	Goals
1931/32	3	1	0	0	1	0
1932/33	10	4	—	—	2	0
1933/34	35	10	2	0	2	0
1934/35	15	4	—	—	4	0
1935/36	18	6	1	0	—	—
1939/40	15	4	—	—	—	—
	96	**29**	**3**	**0**	**9**	**0**

The void League match versus Falkirk on 9 March 1935 has been included as an appearance and his goal in that match has also been included.
1939/40: Wartime Regional League.

Central defender, 1994-1995

Manager Simon Stainrod became intent on bringing a veritable 'Foreign Legion' to the club. It all began with the acquisition of Franck Rolling, a Frenchman, who was easily the best of Stainrod's foreign signings.

Rolling, formerly of FC Pau (France), was close to attaining the age of twenty-six when he arrived at Ayr for pre-season training with a view to signing. He consented to sign in time to go on the club's tour to the Republic of Ireland. Simon Stainrod commented: 'He's a top-class player who can play either centre half or midfield. He played with me in Strasbourg's first team when he was only nineteen and that's exceptional'. It was an accurate assessment. Rolling was soon showing the Ayr support why his new manager defined him as 'top class'.

His competitive debut came with the visit of Hamilton Accies for the opening League fixture of the 1994/95 season. In drawing 1-1, there was no indication of what the immediate future would hold. One week later, the visit of St Mirren brought a further 1-1 scoreline together with the observation that: 'Franck Rolling had another superb performance'. Then began a decline which veered towards rapid, rather than gradual. It should be stressed that the decline referred to related to the team in general and, consequently, results. Rolling was absolved from all blame. In fact he was consistently magnificent, even managing to show some class in fraught circumstances.

Bad though things were, Kilmarnock were beaten 4-1 at Somerset Park on 17 December 1994. Franck Rolling scored the final goal of the match, although nothing more than local pride and the custody of the Ayrshire Cup was at stake. In terms of morale, it was thought that this result would provide the momentum required to climb out of the First Division's basement area. On 2 January 1995, a 2-0 defeat at Stranraer created uproar among the support. It then became vital to beat another struggling club, St Mirren, in the next fixture. With seventeen minutes played, Rolling scored with a twenty-five-yard shot to the delight and relief of the home fans. In the final minute, Brian Bilsland finished it at 2-0, thereby pulling Ayr United to within two points of third-bottom St Mirren. Rolling's contribution extended beyond his goal and his general performance. In the absence of the suspended Hugh Burns, the game was won under his captaincy. It transpired that the temporary captaincy became permanent. On the expiry of his suspension, Hugh Burns had expected to be included for a Tuesday evening fixture against Airdrie at Broadwood Stadium. Simon Stainrod thought otherwise, as he considered Burns to be lacking match fitness. Burns resolved the issue by walking out on the club.

On 11 February 1995, top-placed Dundee lost 1-0 at Ayr, thereby lifting the club marginally clear of the bottom two positions. It was a false dawn. A gradual slide into the Second Division was caused by a lack of quality in the squad. Franck Rolling was far too classy to face playing in the Scottish Second Division. After playing two matches at that level, he went on trial with Leicester City. It was a successful trial and a price of £100,000 was agreed for his transfer.

In 1997 he was a Motherwell trialist in pre-season games, although he opted to join Bournemouth soon afterwards. Further moves involved him going to Gillingham then Wycombe Wanderers.

	League		Scottish Cup		League Cup	
	Apps	Goals	Apps	Goals	Apps	Goals
1994/95	33	2	1	0	1	0
1995/96	2	0	–	–	1	0
	35	2	1	0	2	0

Mention the word 'Viva' to long-standing Ayr United supporters and memories of Bobby Rough will be induced. In the summer of 1969, the song 'Viva Bobby Joe' landed in the UK charts. Ayr United supporters sang the chorus with 'Bobby Joe' substituted by 'Bobby Rough'.

Rough had already established himself at the club, having been signed from Dundee, aged twenty, during the 1968 close season. His first game in front of an Ayr crowd was a pre-season friendly against Halifax Town, a friendly in name only. There was much hard tackling and he suffered. In a 2-2 draw he scored with what was described as 'an unsaveable drive'. One week later, the fans retraced their steps to Somerset Park for the proper start to the season. This involved beating Cowdenbeath 3-1 in a League Cup sectional tie. Rough scored the first goal and, with a great solo effort, the final one.

Ayr United won that League Cup section, thereby qualifying for the quarter-finals. Progress was halted by a 3-0 aggregate defeat against Clyde and this was compounded by Bobby Rough suffering a back injury in the second leg at Shawfield. Five Second Division fixtures were missed. His return was a scoring one, in a 4-1 home win over Forfar Athletic.

Rough's remit was supposedly to create chances from his left-wing beat. He did this to good effect, although he was capable of going beyond the call of duty. On 30 November 1968, he scored a hat-trick when East Stirling were crushed 6-1 at Somerset Park. Winning the Second Division Championship stood to be an insurmountable task in view of Motherwell's quite exceptional form. Promotion as runners-up was most satisfactory. That summer 'Cutty' Young came to the club. Young on the right flank and Rough on the left soon proved potent. In a 3-0 opening League win over Hibs, Rough scored one and created another. In the famous 3-3 draw against Celtic in a Hampden League Cup semi-final, he opened the scoring with a brilliant header and, five minutes into extra time, he again put Ayr United in front with a header. In the replay he laid on the opening goal for Alex Ingram and it was just too bad that defeat had eventually to be conceded.

After a match at Morton on New Year's Day 1970, it was discovered that Bobby Rough had torn knee ligaments. He returned to face Hearts at Tynecastle Park on the first Saturday of March. Alas, it was a premature return. In reality it was the end of his season. Reports that he had been ruled out for the remainder of the campaign were accurate. Thereafter he was only selected occasionally over the course of the next two seasons. On Christmas Day 1971, he was brought back into the first team at left-back, having played there for the reserves. The result was a 1-0 away win over Partick Thistle and he was retained in that position for a 3-0 win away to Morton on New Year's Day 1972. After a run of matches at left-back, Bobby Rough disappeared from first-team contention, and was released at the end of 1972/73.

| | League | | Scottish Cup | | League Cup | |
	Apps	Goals	Apps	Goals	Apps	Goals
1968/69	28	6	2	1	8	4
1969/70	20	3	0	0	10	3
1970/71	9 +3	1	0	0	0	0
1971/72	8 +1	0	0	0	2 +1	0
1972/73	0	0	0	0	0	0
	65	10	2	1	20	7
	+4 sub. listings				+1 sub. listing	

Len Round

Goalkeeper, 1946-1957

Len Round was born in Wall Heath on 21 May 1928. While still a schoolboy in his native West Midlands, he decided that his best position was goalkeeper and his first experience of competitive football came in 1944/45 when he played for Wall Heath Old Boys, a club which was run by his father.

He was called up for national service and joined the Royal Scots Fusiliers. He was posted to a camp in Ayrshire and this was how he got a trial for Ayr United. That trial was in a reserve match against the Kilmarnock counterparts at Somerset Park on 26 October 1946. After a 1-1 draw it was written that: 'In this his reserve debut, Round impressed by his agility, courage and resourcefulness'. On the strength of that performance he was signed.

After several reserve games, he found himself having to serve in India and he did not return until January 1948. On his return, Len Round's first match was a reserve friendly at home to a Celtic team. Then, one week later, came the deferred first-team debut. The date was 7 February 1948 and it was the occasion of Stenhousemuir being crushed 6-0 at Somerset Park. It was to his credit that he completed the season as first-choice goalkeeper. Yet Len felt pangs of homesickness. He was living in digs and working full time at Prestwick St Nicholas Golf Club. In an interview for *Football Monthly* in 1954 he reflected on this phase by stating: 'I began to feel a little homesick and missed my family and friends. I shall be eternally grateful to Mr Ferrier (manager) for his friendship and fatherly counsel.'

In 1955 Len married an Ayr girl and in the 1955/56 season he played in every League match in what amounted to a promotion-winning season. In January 1957 Billy Travers was drafted in to play in the Ayr goal and, despite suffering relegation, his form was so exceptional that he could not be dropped. Nevertheless it still came as a shock when Len Round's name appeared on the list of freed players at the end of that season.

In the summer of 1957 he signed for Hull City and his next move took him to Kent where he played for Sittingbourne for eight years. He returned to his native Wall Heath and then played for Lower Gornal Athletic before deciding to retire from the game at the end of the 1968/69 season, by which time he was aged forty-one. However, during the following season, he helped out in an emergency situation and agreed to play for Wall Heath. The supposed emergency situation carried over into the next again season and he ultimately retired from goalkeeping at the age of forty-three.

	League Apps	Scottish Cup Apps	League Cup Apps
1947/48	8	0	0
1948/49	30	2	6
1949/50	11	1	0
1950/51	30	4	7
1951/52	29	1	2
1952/53	28	2	6
1953/54	29	1	8
1954/55	22	5	8
1955/56	36	2	3
1956/57	19	0	6
	242	18	46

Malcolm Shotton smiled constantly, even in intense pressure during matches. This charismatic approach, combined with his devotion to defending, made him popular with the supporters.

His career took him from Leicester City to Nuneaton Borough and then to Oxford United. He was with Oxford during a meteoric rise from the Third Division to the First Division (pre-Premiership years) and, in his role as captain, had the honour of lifting the Milk Cup at Wembley. Subsequent moves took him to Portsmouth, Huddersfield Town, Barnsley and Hull City. He then briefly assisted Frickley Colliery before signing for Ayr United on 4 September 1992. At this time the assistant manager at Somerset Park was Dale Roberts, who had been at Hull City at the same time as Shotton.

Since the previous match, Willie Furphy had been released. Shotton went straight into the team on the day after signing, and was also given the captaincy. This was the first home match since beating Kilmarnock 2-0 but, this time, the match was conceded to Morton by the same scoreline. By autumn there was an improvement in results – under Shotton's captaincy there had to be. Although he played football with a smile on his face, he was ensured that there was no slacking. His opponents though, were not so ready to smile. When Shotton challenged them, they knew they about it! At this stage of his career, he was a tackler of considerable repute. Yet although he was hard, he was also fair. In his time at Ayr he was shown one red card, in highly dubious circumstances, against Motherwell in a League Cup tie in August 1993.

On the eve of a Scottish Cup tie at Dunfermline in January 1993, an ankle injury rendered it difficult for him even to walk. In desperation he went to paddle in the sea. After further treatment it was decided to take a chance in selecting him. His performance was so good that he won the 'Man of The Match' award. On the day before the next round, he had an injury problem once more. The nature of it was a back complaint which had developed during training. This problem was cleared up by acupuncture!

Being a stopper, goalscoring was not one of his main traits. Curiously though, his three goals for Ayr United were all scored against Morton. The first one was a header in a 2-1 defeat at Cappielow Park on 24 October 1992. A further headed goal at the same venue on 20 November 1993, had differing consequences in that it was the only goal of the match. The other goal was an equaliser in a midweek fixture at Somerset Park on 1 March 1994. Brian Bilsland then hit the winner with four minutes left and created chaotic scenes. Amid the celebrations, a greyhound ran onto the field. Malcolm Shotton was not a speed merchant but caught the dog and carried it off the field!

On Hogmanay 1993, new boss Simon Stainrod named Shotton as his assistant manager. Alas, he accepted another opportunity in July 1994 when he went to Barnsley as a coach; although he was pressed into action as a player in the season ahead. In March 1995 he scored in a 2-0 win over Sunderland to become Barnsley's oldest ever scorer. In January 1998 he departed Barnsley to become manager of Oxford United. On bringing his Oxford team to Ayr for a pre-season friendly in 1999, he received an ovation prior to the kick-off. During the 1999/00 season he left Oxford and his next job in football was as a coach at Bradford City.

	League		Scottish Cup		League Cup	
	Apps	Goals	Apps	Goals	Apps	Goals
1992/93	35	1	2	0	–	–
1993/94	38	2	1	0	1	0
	73	3	3	0	1	0

In the closing days of January 1986, Ally MacLeod had to cope with the problem of a four-match ban for Lex Grant. In pursuit of a solution, he approached Airdrie and arranged a loan deal for John Sludden. He had played for Scotland Schoolboys in a well-remembered 5-4 victory against their English counterparts at Wembley. His senior career had then taken him from Celtic to St Johnstone prior to going to Airdrie. On 1 February 1986, he made his Ayr United debut in a 2-2 draw against Partick Thistle. Then, after taking part in a 1-0 Scottish Cup defeat against Hibs at Easter Road, his first Ayr United goal came in a 1-1 draw at Dumbarton. On the following Saturday, he scored in a 1-0 win over Morton, although no one could have guessed just how good he would become. The loan deal extended until the end of what was a relegation season.

At the start of 1986/87, John Sludden was still an Airdrie player. Then, on 20 August 1986, he was purchased for a mere £5,000. It was a timely transaction. That night there was a Skol Cup tie against Kilmarnock. Sludden scored the first goal in a 2-1 win.

A failure to pick up a point from the concluding League fixture cost the club immediate promotion but Sludden was able to reflect on 30 competitive goals. He was named as the Supporters' Association 'Player of The Year' as well as the Scottish PFA 'Player of the Year' for the Second Division.

On the eve of 1987/88, Henry Templeton joined the club and, in future years, supporters would reminisce on the 'Sludden and Templeton era'. On 26 September 1987, Sludden scored a hat-trick in a 4-1 win at home to Queen's Park. It was his third League hat-trick to this point of the season. Ally MacLeod jokingly said that, in Sludden's case, he would make it five goals in order to keep the ball. The goals and points were piled on as teams became subjected to 'a dose of the Sludds'.

'Sludden rose to send a majestic back-header looping over the head of 'keeper McLafferty. That signalled the start of one big party and with the referee's whistle came a pitch invasion and a mass singsong' – Ayr United 3 Stranraer 1, 9 April 1988. The euphoria was caused by it being the team's 100th competitive goal of the season. A case of champagne had been put up by the *Daily Record* for the first club to reach that total. In winning the Second Division Championship, Sludden netted 31 League goals. Not since Peter Price in 1958/59 had an Ayr United player broken the thirty-goal barrier.

Once back in the First Division, defences were more difficult to unlock. Yet, even although there were fewer opportunities, Sludden was still a dangerous striker.

In mid-August 1989, he broke an ankle in a Skol Cup tie at home to Hamilton Accies. Then, on 18 December that year, he moved back into the Second Division on being sold to Kilmarnock for £50,000. Further moves took him to East Fife, Clydebank, Clyde and Stenhousemuir. In July 1993 he appeared in an Ayr United shirt again, for Ally MacLeod's testimonial against Blackburn Rovers.

His goalscoring was good enough to put him in the club's top-ten all-time scorers.

	League		Scottish Cup		League Cup	
	Apps	Goals	Apps	Goals	Apps	Goals
1985/86	16	5	1	0	–	–
1986/87	37	26	4	3	2	1
1987/88	39	31	4	1	2	0
1988/89	39	15	1	0	1	0
1989/90	6 +4	2	–	–	1	0
	137	79	10	4	6	1
	+4 sub. listings					

Centre forward, 1927-1929

*Jimmy Smith,
seated fourth
player from left.*

If the story of Jimmy Smith was used as a basis for footballing fiction, the publisher would doubtlessly request the writer to tone it down a bit. It is a story of goalscoring abandon. He was born in Old Kilpatrick in 1902 and his career began in his native locality with Dumbarton Harp then Clydebank. Smith next put pen to paper for Rangers from whom he was released in 1927. That summer he scored five in a trial match for Ayr United. Terms were offered and accepted.

After two failed attempts to return to the First Division, the early indications were that 1927/28 would also prove abortive. The first four League matches included a draw and two defeats. It began with a visit from St Bernard's which resulted in a 4-4 draw, although Jimmy Smith was able to distinguish himself with a hat-trick. Yet in the months ahead a hat-trick was to prove a routine accomplishment for him. In the season's fifth League match, the Somerset Park crowd witnessed Smith score all the Ayr goals in a 5-3 win over Albion Rovers. He scored all five in the first half! It was a performance which prompted the following comments: 'A tireless worker and a first-class opportunist, Smith, barring accidents, will score many goals for his new club.' It was an accurate prophecy.

A 2-0 away win over Morton in mid-October took Ayr United to the top of the Second Division table and the position remained unassailed. It was observed that: 'The ball was tapped from man to man with machine-like precision.' Smith did not score in that match but it was apparent that his supreme ability to lead the line was inspiring confidence throughout the team.

In response to an away hat-trick over East Stirling in early December, a further prophecy surfaced: 'If he maintains anything like his present shooting form he will create a record that will be hard to beat.' At this time the individual record in Britain comprised the 59 League goals scored by George Camsell for Middlesbrough the season before. However Dixie Dean stood to complete the 1927/28 season with sixty League goals for Everton. Alec Troup, formerly a guest player with Ayr United, provided the cross for goal number sixty. Jimmy Smith had 35 League goals to his credit by the turn of the year.

As expected, he was the subject of special attention from opposition defenders but this still did not stifle his goalscoring menace. Against East Stirling, he equalled Camsell's record in the course of a 2-1 home win on 7 April 1928. He then had thirty minutes in which to break the record and he was constantly plied with the ball in pursuit of the sixtieth goal. It took heavy marking to prevent him from getting what would have been his third goal of the afternoon. The honour was deferred merely two days. On a Monday afternoon, during a 3-3 draw with Third Lanark at Cathkin Park, he scored to beat Camsell's record then scored again to eclipse the total which Dixie Dean was on the verge of reaching. By the end of the season his total had risen to 66 League goals, an achievement noted in *The Guinness Book Of Records*.

In an end of season tour to Scandinavia he scored ten, including two in Ayr United's 3-1 defeat of the Swedish international team in Stockholm. Scandinavian newspapers referred to him as 'the British champion'.

Replicating such prolific goalscoring in the First Division was not likely to happen but the goals still flowed with regularity. On 10 November 1928, Ayr United trailed 4-2 away to Partick Thistle at half-time. The result was Partick Thistle 4 Ayr United 8. Jimmy Smith scored five, four of which were in the second half.

For an undisclosed transfer fee which was stated to be 'considerable', Jimmy Smith signed for Liverpool on Wednesday 18 September 1929. That Saturday he scored twice in a win over Manchester United.

Further moves took him to Tunbridge Wells, Bristol Rovers, Newport County, Notts County and then Dumbarton as player-manager then manager. He eventually emigrated to the United States where he died in 1975.

Jimmy Smith's Goalscoring Record: 1927/28.

League

Date	Opponents	Goals Scored
13-8-27	St Bernard's (home)	3
27-8-27	Alloa Athletic (home)	2
10-9-27	Albion Rovers (home)	5
24-9-27	Forfar Athletic (home)	3
6-10-27	Clydebank (away)	3
22-10-27	Arbroath (away)	1
29-10-27	East Fife (home)	1
5-11-27	Third Lanark (home)	2
26-11-27	Armadale (home)	3
3-12-27	East Stirling (away)	3
10-12-27	Dundee United (away)	1
17-12-27	Leith Athletic (home)	2
24-12-27	St Bernard's (away)	2
31-12-27	Arthurlie (home)	4
2-1-28	Morton (home)	2
7-1-28	Alloa Athletic (away)	3
14-1-28	Bathgate (home)	5
28-1-28	Queen of the South (away)	2
8-2-28	Clydebank (home)	1
11-2-28	Forfar Athletic (away)	1
25-2-28	Arbroath (home)	4
3-3-28	King's Park (home)	2
17-3-28	Stenhousemuir (home)	1
31-3-28	Armadale (away)	1
7-4-28	East Stirling (home)	2
9-4-28	Third Lanark (away)	2
14-4-28	Dundee United (home)	4
21-4-28	Leith Athletic (away)	1

Total: 66

Scottish Cup

21-1-28	Bo'ness (home)	2

Total: 2

Friendlies

4-1-28	Stranraer (away)	1
10-3-28	Workington (away)	2

Total: 3

Ayr Charity Cup

5-5-28	Kilmarnock (home)	1

Total: 1

Scandinavian Tour

22-5-28	Gjoa	1
24-5-28	Sweden	2
27-5-28	Gzoa Crana	3
?-6-28	Ooestfold	4

Total: 10

These statistics may give the illusion of belonging to an entire team. In reality it is one man's scoring record for one season.

Jock Smith was a Beith farmer boy whose nickname reflected his occupation. He was known as 'Fermer' Smith in the Scottish vernacular. Smith was signed as a right-back from Neilston Victoria in August 1919. Initially, though, he was played as a winger, no doubt on account of his speed. At the time of his signing he was described as 'a noted runner'.

Ayr United got an early dividend on his £10 signing-on fee. On the evening of 3 September 1919 he made his debut in a 1-1 draw at home to Raith Rovers. He retained the outside left position and got his first goals for the club precisely a fortnight later. That was in a 4-0 home win over Albion Rovers against whom he scored twice. Albion Rovers were destined to go on and compete in that season's Scottish Cup final. Three days later Kilmarnock, who would win that season's Scottish Cup, came to Somerset Park. The midweek win was eclipsed with a 5-0 victory in the Ayrshire derby in which Smith again scored. Tellingly, reports of the Kilmarnock match were peppered with his name, thereby indicating a high level of involvement.

It is a gratifying statistic that Ayr United were able to field a forward line containing four players who were either present or future Scotland internationals. These players were Johnny Crosbie, Jimmy Richardson, Neil McBain and, of course, Jock Smith. The other forward, Billy Middleton, was ineligible to play for Scotland due to his roots in County Durham while a further pertinent point is that

Phil McCloy and Jimmy Hogg of this team would also be capped at a future date. In hindsight it may be considered that Smith's potential as a full-back should have been identified sooner. Yet this argument must be countered with the fact that he was a star winger with an eye for goal. Furthermore he displayed facets which could define him as the ultimate utility player. This was glaringly the case when chosen to play at left-back at home to Morton on 13 December 1919 when Phil McCloy, the usual incumbent, was missing through injury. It was noted that: 'He had not long begun when he showed he knew all about the full-back game'. At half-time a 2-0 lead was held, a fragile margin when weighed against George Nisbet's non-appearance for the second half. Jock Smith gamely donned the goalkeeper's sweater and the 2-0 scoreline was preserved to the end. One of Smith's saves was described as 'really brilliant'. This was just one week before the famous Smith and McCloy full-back partnership was fielded for the first time. Even then it did not become a regular partnership until regular right-back John Semple was sold to Luton Town for £200 in the summer of 1920.

On New Year's Day 1923, a scoreless draw was played out against Morton at Cappielow Park and a journalist paid a glowing tribute to the Ayr United full-backs: 'Smith and McCloy never made a mistake'.

The England v. Scotland international of 1924 was the first international played at Wembley. On that occasion Smith and McCloy were the Scotland full-backs and, after a 1-1 draw, The *Bulletin* wrote: 'The Beith farmer kept plodding on and generally created a fine impression. He kicked powerfully and with accuracy and the longer the game lasted the better did he become.'

Jock Smith did not win a further full international cap and a contributory factor had to be Ayr United's pending relegation in the season ahead. That was also his testimonial season. His benefit match was contested at Beresford Park on 17 September 1924 when he scored with a penalty kick in a 1-1 draw against Kilmarnock.

Phil McCloy's departure in August 1925 caused Smith to become a regular in the vacated left-back position. Predictably there was speculation about Smith also moving to England. Counter speculation noted that his farming ties would prevent such a move. His marriage in 1925 further implied that he would settle in Ayrshire. After a 2-0 home win over Armadale on 5 September 1925, he was presented with 'a handsome armchair' from his teammates. Captain Bobby Stewart handed it over. Further recognition came when he represented the Scottish League at left-back against the Football League at Celtic Park on 13 March 1926. He was not wholly forgotten in the Second Division.

Jock Smith did not sign on for season 1926/27 and the old argument that farming life would prevent him moving from Beith was no longer valid. One of the two farms owned by the family had been disposed of. This made it less urgent for him to remain and help his father. On Friday 3 September 1926 (precisely seven years after his debut) he signed for Middlesbrough.

With Middlesbrough he won Second Division Championship medals in 1927 and 1929. In September 1930 he moved to Cardiff City where he won a Welsh Cup winner's medal while a further move to Distillery saw him as an Irish Cup finalist in 1933. The significance of the Distillery move was that he developed an affinity for Northern Ireland and settled there. In April 1973 Ayr United received news from Ireland that Jock Smith had died.

	League		Ayr Charity Cup		Scottish Cup	
	Apps	Goals	Apps	Goals	Apps	Goals
1919/20	33	10	1	0	3	0
1920/21	37	0	1	0	5	0
1921/22	40	0	1	0	2	0
1922/23	36	0	1	0	3	0
1923/24	27	1	0	0	7	0
1924/25	36	0	1	0	2	0
1925/26	36	6	1	0	1	0
	245	17	6	0	23	0

Peter Smith
Wing half, 1938-1940, 1945-1948

In the summer of 1938 it was considered that the Ayr United half-back line should be strengthened. To this end the prime target was Scot Symon, who had been transferred from Dundee to Portsmouth in 1935. The player did opt to return to Scotland but his move took him to Rangers. Attention turned to Peter Smith, a nineteen-year-old left half with a club called Scottish Dyes. On Tuesday 13 September 1938, Smith agreed to sign and he made a reserve debut against Clyde reserves at Shawfield that night. In November a journalist expressed the following opinion on the Ayr United team: 'It is the most sound to don Somerset Park colours for quite a few years.' It was a view which probably contained the reason for Smith's first-team debut being deferred until 25 February 1939 when Hibs were beaten 3-2 at Easter Road.

Smith's inclusion was at the expense of Jock Mayes but, for the rest of the season, Peter Smith was played at right half with Mayes being switched to the left and Davy Currie remaining at centre half. Season 1939/40 should have been his first complete campaign but, after the declaration of war, Smith was the first Ayr United player to go on military service. There still existed an opportunity to play football while on leave although, from the summer of 1940, it was not possible to do so at Ayr.

In the last wartime season he played for Pollok Juniors. Then, on Ayr United's resurrection, he returned to the club having been on the retained list throughout the hostilities. VE Day was on 8 May 1945 and VJ Day followed on 15 August. On the Saturday prior to VJ Day the club reappeared for a League match against Airdrie at Somerset Park. A 3-0 defeat was suffered although a five-year absence rendered it excusable. John Malcolm, at centre forward, had been a teammate of Peter Smith at Pollok Juniors. At a future date they would also be reunited as teammates at East Stirling.

On 13 October 1945, Ayr United were the highest away scorers in League football in Britain on that day. The victims were Stenhousemuir. In the course of a 6-0 rout Peter Smith scored with a forty-yard drive. One week later, in a 1-1 draw at home to Raith Rovers, he scored an equaliser which was described as 'a brilliant solo goal'. Enhancing his scoring status further was his emerging reputation as a 'penalty king'.

Smith was an influential player. This assertion can be evidenced by his being made captain. Further proof is the mention of his name when fans are reminiscing about the post-war era. On 3 January 1948 the visit of East Fife saw six goals shared and it was the last time he pulled on an Ayr United shirt. Within days he had been released at his own request and immediately joined East Stirling.

A further move took him to Stenhousemuir for whom he appeared in a League Cup tie at Ayr as late as 1 September 1956.

	League		Scottish Cup		League Cup	
	Apps	Goals	Apps	Goals	Apps	Goals
1938/39	9	0	0	0	–	–
1939/40	6	1	–	–	–	–
1945/46	21	7	–	–	8	1
1946/47	20	0	2	0	3	2
1947/48	3	0	–	–	6	0
	59	8	2	0	17	3

1939/40: First Division (2), Wartime Regional League (4).

Hugh Sproat

Goalkeeper, 1974-1979, 1984-1986

Of all the great showmen ever to have played for Ayr United, Hugh Sproat is up there with the best of them. In common with the club's other extroverts, he had the ability to match.

He started off with Heathside Amateurs before moving on to Maybole Juniors then Auchinleck Talbot. In October 1974, Ayr United made an approach and an agreement was reached whereby he was to join whenever Auchinleck could find a replacement. During that same month, Ally McLean, the regular custodian, was injured and there was speculation that Hugh Sproat would be called upon to play at Airdrie. Ian McGiffen, aged seventeen, was pressed into action in that match and he retained his place pending McLean's return in February 1975, by which time Sproat was starring for the reserves. After appearing in a friendly in which Ayr United beat a strong Celtic team 2-0, he was considered ready for a competitive appearance. His debut came in the next match; a 1-0 win over Airdrie on 1 March 1975. The jersey was then his regularly.

His first complete season was in the new Premier League. In the preceding League Cup sectional ties, Sproat's form was inspirational. That form was maintained in the League programme. On October 11 1975, he picked up an early injury during a visit from Rangers. Despite his discomfort being visible, he played on in a 3-0 victory. In 1975/76 there was a last-game escape and the next season saw the club pull clear after some resurgent form in March and April, after Hugh Sproat had reclaimed his place from Andy Geoghegan. Although relegated in 1978, it was no reflection on Sproat who was the Supporters' Association 'Player of The Year'.

In 1978/79, he missed just one League fixture; against Dumbarton on 16 September 1978. That morning he had wrenched his back while lifting a crate during his milk round. Richard Northcote deputised in goal though he was injured and had already been ruled unfit to play for the reserves. Northcote struggled in a 5-2 defeat. The result created public ire and manager Alex Stuart resigned. Ally MacLeod quit the Scotland job to manage Ayr United again and Jock Stein quit Leeds United to take the Scotland post. Cesar Luis Menotti was mentioned as a contender for the vacancy at Leeds. That appointment did not take place but, had the speculation been accurate, world champions Argentina would have lost their manager due to Sproat hurting himself during a milk round.

During the 1979 close season, Hugh Sproat was signed for Motherwell by Ally MacLeod. In return Ayr United received Stewart Rennie, Jimmy Lindsay and a cash adjustment. In summer 1984, now thirty-one, he rejoined Ayr United on being released by Motherwell. His second spell lasted for two seasons and his tricks were still there, including ball-juggling during stoppages, concluding the performance with a back-heel into his own net, conducting opposition choirs, wearing tracksuit trousers in warm weather and bowing after being applauded.

	League Apps	Scottish Cup Apps	League Cup Apps
1974/75	11	0	—
1975/76	36	3	6
1976/77	15	2	5
1977/78	28	1	4
1978/79	38	2	6
1984/85	37	2	2
1985/86	24	2	0
	189	12	23

Davy Stewart
Goalkeeper, 1967-1973

Davy Stewart played for the Kilsyth Rangers team which won the Scottish Junior Cup in 1967. That summer, at the age of twenty, he signed for Ayr United. It did not take long for him to become known as 'The Man In Black'.

His debut came at Stranraer in a League Cup sectional tie which was won 4-1. 'Stewart had a brilliant game, particularly during the period of late pressure' – St Mirren 1 Ayr United 2, 30 August 1967. 'Stewart had a great double save from a penalty by Hopper' – Queen's Park 1 Ayr United 1, 11 November 1967. Such performances became routine. His handling was so good that he had an ability to hold fierce shots with seeming ease.

In October 1969, a harsh 2-1 Hampden defeat against Celtic in a League Cup semi-final replay, saw opposing goalkeeper Ronnie Simpson emerge as the player who did most to influence the outcome. However that tie, and the original one, proved that Davy Stewart had the strength of character to keep his composure in high profile matches. 'Donald Ford blasted a terrific shot which brought out a miraculous diving save from Stewart' – Ayr United 0 Hearts 0, 18 October 1969. Such form earned him a place in the Scotland Under-23 squad for a game against France at Hampden on 3 December 1969. Teammate Dick Malone played in the match but, on this occasion, Tommy Hughes of Chelsea played in goal. His chance was deferred merely until

14 January 1970 when he played for the Under-23 team in a 1-1 draw against the Welsh at Aberdeen.

During the 1971 close season, Stewart was out of contract and would not sign. When the competitive fixtures began, Jim Gilmour was still guarding the Ayr United goal. After missing three League Cup sectional ties, Stewart relented and put pen to paper. 'Stewart was in great form' – Ayr United 0 Celtic 1, 30 October 1971. He was emphatically back.

The momentum of 1972/73 rolled into 1973/74. These were days in which Ayr United became established as a force. The form of Davy Stewart was consistent with that of the team in general. 'Stewart was in brilliant form' – Hibs 1 Ayr United 0, 15 August 1970. On 19 September 1973, Leicester City drew 1-1 at Ayr in a first round tie in the Texaco Cup. The visiting goalkeeper was Peter Shilton who, realistically, had the reputation of being the best goalkeeper in the world at the time. A fortnight later, Davy Stewart did not play in the second leg at Leicester. In the interim period he had been sold to Leeds United for £30,000. On 9 January 1974, he made his Leeds debut in a 1-0 win over Wolves in the FA Cup. Davy Stewart played for Leeds United against Bayern Munich in the 1975 European Cup final and won a full Scotland cap in 1977.

In November 1978 he was sold to West Bromwich Albion for £70,000 and a further move took him to Swansea City in February 1980. In the summer of 1982, he moved to Hong Kong to play for Ryoden FC but he returned to settle in Swansea.

	League Apps	Scottish Cup Apps	League Cup Apps
1967/68	36	1	10
1968/69	35	2	8
1969/70	34	1	10
1970/71	31	1	6
1971/72	22	3	3
1972/73	30	4	3
1973/74	5	–	6
	193	12	46

Gary Teale's form with Clydebank ensured that his name was often subject to transfer speculation. While other clubs dithered, Ayr United moved in with an £85,000 offer which secured his signature on 2 October 1998. One day after signing, he appeared in a First Division fixture at St Mirren. He fitted in nicely in a 2-0 win, despite not having trained with his teammates.

Gary Teale was a pacey midfielder. He excelled in this role on his home debut a fortnight later. On that occasion he scored the opening goal of a 4-2 win over Falkirk. On 14 November, the top of the First Division was reached with a 4-1 win over Clydebank, and the position was reinforced with a 2-0 win at Airdrie a week later. Teale again scored.

The purchase of Teale was exceptional business, given his form and his age (twenty). Then it all came to a halt when he was substituted at Falkirk on 5 December 1998, the problem a pulled hamstring. The injury rendered him unavailable until reappearing in a 4-0 win over Stranraer on 2 January 1999. This was not the only comfortable win in that month. In eliminating Kilmarnock from the Scottish Cup, the final goal in a 3-0 win had come from a penalty awarded after Gary Teale had been brought down. In full flight, he was hard to stop by legal means.

On the evening of 27 April 1999, Ayr United played in front of the lowest ever recorded attendance for a competitive match involving the club. For a League fixture against Clydebank at Dumbarton's Boghead Park, the crowd figure numbered three short of 200. On the same night, Gary Teale was in Germany where he went on as a substitute for the Scotland Under-21 team in a 2-1 loss. In total he would receive six caps at that level,

these being evenly divided between his time at Clydebank and Ayr United. In 2004 he was included in the full Scotland squad.

'Straight from the kick-off Gary Teale was released and he set off on a run which saw him beat three defenders before crossing... and Neil Tarrant rose to head past Ally Maxwell for a goal timed at twenty seconds' – Ayr United 3 Morton 2, 5 February 2000. By two seconds this was a club record and it was down to Teale's speed. Three weeks later, Tarrant and Teale evenly shared the Ayr goals in a 4-3 Scottish Cup win at Motherwell.

In 2000/01, the improved League form was reflected in the form of Gary Teale. None of his skills were superfluous. He always looked committed to bearing down on goal by the shortest available route.

In July 2001, Gary Teale, although not scoring, was involved in three of the goals when Wigan Athletic lost 4-0 at Ayr in a pre-season friendly. In December of the same year he was sold to... Wigan Athletic! It was a successful move since Wigan won promotion to the Nationwide League First Division in 2002/03. That success enabled more money to come the way of Ayr United. Teale's sale had included add-ons for appearances and promotion. By such clauses, the up-front amount of £275,000 was supplemented to exceed £400,000. It therefore became the highest transfer fee ever received by the club.

	League		Scottish Cup		League Cup	
	Apps	Goals	Apps	Goals	Apps	Goals
1998/99	23	4	4	1	–	–
1999/00	26 +6	0	5	2	1 +1	0
2000/01	27 +2	5	1	0	1	0
2001/02	18	4	–	–	3	1
	94	13	10	3	5	1
	+8 sub. listings				+1 sub. listing	

On the evening before the first competitive match of 1987/88, the Ayr United board agreed to part with £6,000 for the purchase of Henry Templeton from Airdrie. It was the second time the player had signed for Ally MacLeod and it was not to be the last time. While in charge at Airdrie, Ally had fixed him up from Shettleston Juniors.

Templeton was pitched straight into the team to face St Johnstone in a Second Division fixture at Perth, the next day. It ended in a scoreless draw and a season was to unfold in which both clubs were to achieve what amounted to, at the time, a club record points total.

On 14 December 1985, Templeton had destroyed Ayr United with a hat-trick in a 4-0 Airdrie win at Ayr. From August 1987 onwards he was to wreak much more havoc at Somerset Park. Mercifully he did so while wearing a white shirt and black shorts. He was a small jinking winger in the traditional Scottish mould and was possessed of the type of natural skills which cannot be coached into a player.

'Templeton was the star performer on the synthetic surface' – Stirling Albion 1 Ayr United 1, 5 September 1987. That draw was the preliminary to eight consecutive League wins in which he, together with John Sludden and Tommy Walker, subjected opponents to a goalscoring frenzy. The week after the Stirling match just referred to, a 6-1 win was recorded at Cowdenbeath. In the course of that fixture, Henry Templeton beat three defenders then drove the ball home between two outfield players stationed on the line. This was the kind of form which persistently prompted the fans to sing his name to the tune of the 'Westminster chimes'. Each chorus of 'Henry, Henry, Henry, Henry' was sung with increasing glee. 'Stenhousemuir at times looked resigned to being overwhelmed' – Stenhousemuir 0 Ayr United 6, 3 October 1987. It was turning into a familiar story. Away matches were like road shows and Ally MacLeod had even to voice concern over pitch invasions by over enthusiastic fans. The outstanding results and high enthusiasm were largely attributed to the menacing power of Henry Templeton on the right and Jim Cowell on the left. 'The inspiration for victory again came from Templeton's wizardry' – East Stirling 0 Ayr United 2, 24 October 1987. Saturdays could not come quickly enough.

Backed by a large vocal support, Ayr United went to Dunfermline for a third-round Scottish Cup tie in 1988. Despite a two-league gap, the match was drawn 1-1 but it was almost won. It was observed that: 'Henry Templeton again displayed his brilliant individual skills'. The replay was lost, although there was the substantial consolation that the pursuit of the Second Division Championship remained on its successful course. At the end of that season he succeeded John Sludden as the Scottish PFA 'Player of The Year' for the Second Division. With 23 League goals, he was the Second Division's second-top goalscorer for the season. He was beaten only by his teammate Sludden.

Ally MacLeod loved his teams to have an attacking flair and he certainly had the players to fit that profile. On returning to the First Division, the second League fixture of 1988/89 was away to Meadowbank Thistle. The bus broke down on the way to the stadium and Ally MacLeod ordered Henry Templeton out to undergo a fitness test. This involved him running up and down a pavement in Edinburgh's Haymarket area. When the story leaked, something must have been lost in the translation since it was wrongly reported that the fitness test had taken place amongst bemused shoppers in the city's Princes Street. Templeton then scored the second Ayr goal in a 2-1 victory.

'Templeton brilliantly controlled the ball on his knee before clipping a right-foot volley into McCulloch's top left-hand corner' – Ayr United 4 Kilmarnock 1, 3 January 1989. The team's momentum of the season before failed to carry itself into the First Division but there were still some exceptional results. Templeton scored a later goal too and brought some New Year cheer in the process. The club got sucked into a relegation fight and the skills of Henry Templeton were no less diminished by the urgency of win-or-else matches. The penultimate League fixture brought Airdrie to Somerset Park and it was necessary to win in order to ensure First Division survival. Amid silence, the visitors scored twenty-eight seconds after the kick-off. Henry Templeton then set about playing what seemed to be the game of his life. In a 3-1 win he scored twice, including the final goal in the final minute. Great anxiety gave way to great elation with that last strike.

In the season ahead, the team was once more made to battle in the wrong area of the First Division table. Again though, the

Henry Templeton faces up to his Dundee opponents in the B&Q Centenary Cup final at Motherwell in November 1990.

adverse results were punctuated by days when things came gloriously right. On 2 December 1989, while trailing 1-0 away to Partick Thistle, Templeton stepped up the pace and scored twice (on seventy-three and seventy-nine minutes) for a splendid 2-1 win. In scoring his second goal, he beat three defenders inside the penalty area.

In February 1991, the month after George Burley became manager, he was sold to Clydebank. In a further move, Ally MacLeod signed him for the third time. By that time he was the boss at Queen of the South.

Henry Templeton has since made return visits to Somerset Park in order to do the half-time draw. On each occasion he has been given an ovation.

	League		Scottish Cup		League Cup	
	Apps	Goals	Apps	Goals	Apps	Goals
1987/88	39	23	4	3	2	1
1988/89	33	17	1	1	1	1
1989/90	31 +2	7	2	0	1	0
1990/91	11 +9	0	0	0	1	0
	114	47	7	4	5	2
	+11 sub. listings					

Frank Thompson

Manager, 1935-1940

Frank Thompson was born at Ballynahinch, County Down, on 2 October 1888. His football career blossomed in his native country with the quaintly named Black Diamonds, Cliftonville and Linfield. Thompson next moved to Bradford City where, in his first season, he had the distinction of playing on the wing in their successful FA Cup final team of 1911. In 1913 he was transferred to Clyde. While a Clyde player, he won the last of his 12 caps for Ireland. There is no doubt that he would have made more international appearances had it not been for the intervention of war. That interruption took him away from football for three-and-a-half years, during which he saw military service at the Dardanelles and in Egypt and Salonica.

In November 1922, he made the transformation from Clyde player to player-manager. The managerial role lasted in excess of twelve years and he then moved to take up a similar post at Somerset Park, where a vacancy had arisen due to the resignation of Alex Gibson. On 5 January 1935, a dreadful 8-0 debacle had been suffered away to Albion Rovers. Gibson quit on the Monday. Precisely two weeks later, Thompson took over.

There was a major issue to be addressed since the club remained deep in the relegation mire, largely by dint of a 'goals against' column which would read '112' at the season's end. A last day escape was pulled off. One year later there was to be no such reprieve.

In season 1936/37, the Second Division could not contain Frank Thompson's all-conquering Ayr United team. Apart from breaking the club record for League goals scored in a season, another record was created which stands to this day. This was a run of twelve consecutive League wins. In 1911/12 the club had gone through the League season and won every home League fixture with the exception of one draw. This record was replicated in 1936/37 when the solitary home point dropped came at a time when Frank

Thompson was not there. He spent most of March 1937 in a Prestwick nursing home and, on being discharged, his state of health saw him being confined to his bed at home. Eddie Summers, Albert Smith and Jock Mayes had been signed in October 1936, all of whom Thompson had fixed up for Clyde.

A close flirtation with relegation in 1938 preceded a season in which relegation was comfortably staved off, albeit that no major impression was made on the First Division table. In signing Terry McGibbons and Jacky Cox from Preston North End there was a strong indication that loftier ambitions were being harboured for season 1939/40. The question of how the experience of these players would complement the emerging Hugh McConnell and Lewis Thow would never be answered.

After the declaration of war, Regional Leagues were soon in operation and Frank Thompson was able to obtain the services of Tommy Robertson and Fally Rodger, both former Ayr United greats. George Hamilton, a forward who would have a great career with Aberdeen and Scotland, was called upon to play for Ayr United due to working in Irvine, the town of his birth. In terms of available players the international situation could, and did, work in Frank Thompson's favour at this time but non-availability, even at short notice, more than counterbalanced this.

On 1 June 1940, chairman Andrew Wright was presented with the Scottish Second Eleven Cup at the conclusion of Ayr United's second leg in the final, at home to Aberdeen. With first teams competing, interest should have been high. In reality the crowd did not exceed 3,000. People had more to worry about. The Dunkirk evacuation was in progress. Jock Newall of the Royal Engineers was in that evacuation. He had played for Ayr United that season. These were clearly abnormal times and the club was closed down for the duration thereby rendering Frank Thompson temporarily unemployed.

Although returning to Ireland to manage Glentoran, he did not settle in the land of his birth. His home was in Ayr's Oswald Road at the time of his death on 4 October 1950, just two days after his sixty-second birthday.

After taking part in two trial matches, Bobby Thomson signed for Ayr United on 21 July 1951. He was aged twenty-three at the time and was departing from Craigmark Burntonians. His debut came in a League Cup sectional tie in which Dumbarton were beaten 5-0 at Somerset Park.

Despite making appearances early in the season, he did not establish himself in the first team in that initial season. In time, though, he was to develop into a tough-tackling full-back with a good appetite for the game. The last game in his first season was a friendly at home to Queen's Park Rangers and, curiously, he was selected at centre forward. After losing 2-1 the experiment was never repeated.

It must have been frustrating for Bobby Thomson in those early years at the club. Various full-back partnerships were toyed with while he drifted in and out of the first team. That changed in 1955/56 when he appeared in all of Ayr United's competitive matches. The overall consistency in team selection was a major factor in the successful promotion bid.

In 1958/59 the Second Division Championship was won in addition to promotion, yet it was a chequered season for Thomson. Following a 3-2 win at home to Queen's Park on 5 October 1958, he missed the next eleven League games through having to fight back after injury. However he did succeed in making an unusual contribution to that campaign. When Hamilton Accies visited on 21 March 1959, Sam McMillan opened the scoring. The equaliser was unfortunate inasmuch as it was conceded by way of a Bobby Thomson own goal. Scoring was not his forte but he succeeded in atoning gloriously. With the score standing at 3-1, and just three minutes remaining, he crashed home a free-kick from forty yards. It was an historic goal quite apart from the quality of the strike. That was because it amounted to League goal number 100 for the season. That evening Ayr United were top of the Second Division with eight games remaining, having played twenty-eight matches, winning twenty-four, drawing two and losing only two. The team had amassed fifty points.

At the conclusion of 1960/61, the club faced the prospect of returning to Second Division football. It was an exile which was to extend to five years, although the fight to regain lost ground did not include Bobby Thomson, who was released after ten seasons at the club. It had been a winning start in 1951 and his exit in 1961 was also successful. His final match was the penultimate League fixture of the season, a 3-0 victory at home to Dundee United. The team on that afternoon was: Gallacher, Burn, Thomson, W. McIntyre, Glen, Curlett, Fulton, Gibson, Christie, A. McIntyre, Bradley.

He passed away in 1997.

	League		Scottish Cup		League Cup	
	Apps	Goals	Apps	Goals	Apps	Goals
1951/52	5	0	0	0	5	0
1952/53	12	0	0	0	0	0
1953/54	1	0	0	0	6	0
1954/55	10	0	1	0	5	0
1955/56	36	1	2	0	6	0
1956/57	30	1	1	0	2	0
1957/58	27	0	2	0	6	0
1958/59	17	1	2	0	2	0
1959/60	16	0	3	0	6	0
1960/61	20	0	0	0	4	0
	174	3	11	0	42	0

Lewis Thow
Outside left, 1938-1940, 1945-1946

Lewis Thow first achieved football prominence at school with Newton Park. On 8 April 1933 he played for Scotland schoolboys in an international against Wales. He then played against Ireland and England for a grand slam of appearances in the series. One year later he again played all three internationals.

Lewis Thow played for Ayr United reserves in September 1935 aged fifteen. Subsequently he played junior football with Ardeer Recreation and, on 8 January 1938, he was again fielded for the reserves. The occasion this time was an Alliance League fixture against Rangers reserves at Somerset Park. After a 4-3 win it was observed that 'Thow scintillated on the left wing'. His performance was spoken highly of by a visiting director. What would a director know? In this case, a lot! It was Alan Morton, one of the greatest left-wingers Scottish football has ever known.

Thow was retained in the Alliance League team for a fixture at Beith, by which time he was an Ayr United player. Afterwards he was praised for being 'clever on the ball' and possessing 'strong and direct shooting'. These qualities brought him a first-team debut. It was at Hamilton Accies on 29 January 1938. Thow scored twice in a 3-0 win to become the youngest player to have scored a competitive goal for Ayr United, aged 17 years 293 days. This record stood until 2 March 1993 when Barry Scott, aged 17 years 248 days, also scored against Hamilton Accies on his debut. The record was again broken by Stewart Kean scoring on his debut at Livingston on 29 April 2000, aged 17 years 56 days.

There was little respite from important games. Dundee visited Somerset Park for the concluding League game of 1937/38 and at least a draw was required for survival while the visitors had to win. In a scoreless draw, Thow created opportunities by cutting through and sending over searching crosses. He was unlucky to hit the crossbar in the first-half.

In the summer of 1938 his former colleague Hugh McConnell was signed from Kilwinning Rangers. McConnell broke into the first team at outside right. With McConnell and Thow on the right and left wings they scored 9 and 10 League goals respectively in 1938/39.

At the conclusion of 1939/40, Ayr United beat Aberdeen 3-2 on aggregate in the final of the Scottish Second Eleven Cup. In the first leg Lewis Thow scored in a 1-1 draw at Pittodrie. The particular relevance of this was that first teams competed in that season's competition. Five years then passed before Ayr United next played. Consequently, Thow signed for Morton in December 1940. His registration was still held by Ayr United but he made 2 first-team appearances in 1945/46 having not been demobbed until November 1945. He later played for Newton Stewart.

His most important contribution had yet to be made. In November 1964 news leaked that the directors were considering selling Somerset Park to clear debts. It would have meant killing off Ayr United. Furthermore the story was true. In January 1965 a group of new directors brought stability to the club and extinction was avoided. Thow was one of that group and, in time, became club chairman.

	League		Ayr Charity Cup		Scottish Cup	
	Apps	Goals	Apps	Goals	Apps	Goals
1937/38	6	3	1	0	3	0
1938/39	23	10	–	–	1	0
1939/40	19	1	–	–	–	–
1945/46	2	0	–	–	–	–
	50	14	1	0	4	0

1939/40: First Division (4), Wartime Regional League (15).

Danny Tolland was an immensely popular ball player whom Ayr United signed from Shettleston Juniors. His lively wit ensured that he was just as popular in the dressing room as he was with the fans. Quite simply he was an extrovert. In later years there were older fans who went so far as to insist that Danny Tolland was the greatest player who ever appeared for Ayr United.

In his earliest matches he was selected at centre forward and his debut on 17 January 1925 ended in a 2-1 home defeat against Cowdenbeath. Yet the gloom lifted a week later when the fans retraced their steps to Somerset Park for a Scottish Cup tie in which Tolland scored twice in a 3-1 defeat of St Johnstone. He remained a first-team regular due to being a ball artist who had a great skill at creating openings.

Danny Tolland's first complete season at senior level was, regretfully, in the Second Division. Throughout 1925/26 and 1926/27 there was much experimentation with regard to the selection at centre forward and Tolland himself played a significant number of matches in that position. Yet this was not his best position. His style of play was crying out for a striker with whom he could ply the ball. It is true that he knew the route to goal but his forte was his creativity. Then, in the summer of 1927, Ayr United signed Jimmy Smith whose predatory instinct beautifully complemented the creativity of Danny Tolland. A perfect example of this was the Second Division fixture against Albion Rovers at Somerset Park on 10 September 1927. Smith scored all of the Ayr goals in a 5-3 win and a journalist noted that 'Tolland played one of his best games'.

Admittedly, though, he could be infuriating. On 14 April 1928, Dundee United were annihilated 7-1 at Ayr while the club coasted towards the Second Division title. It was correctly considered that, with some more application, a record score might have been run up. That this did not happen was because 'Tolland and one or two others thought the occasion suitable for a display of trick work'. Almost by way of contradiction the same report had earlier said: 'Tolland's fantastic toe bewildered the Tannadice men'.

Jimmy Smith was transferred to Liverpool in September 1929. However Smith's departure had no adverse affect on Tolland's style. In August 1930, Ayr United sent a team to open Dalbeattie Star's new ground. The 5-2 win was incidental. A more pertinent point is that 'Tolland delighted the crowd'. Delighting the crowd was what he enjoyed best, although there were times when he showed that he could be direct. In other words he was capable of unleashing scoring shots from long range.

In 1928 the player's penchant for sand-dancing had been cited as a reason for Ayr United not reaching double figures against Dundee United but there was glorious atonement on 17 January 1931. In scoring a hat-trick in an 11-2 Scottish Cup rout of Clackmannan, he was eclipsed in the matter of goals by Charlie McGillivray. However Tolland's performance solicited the following praise: 'Tolland was more the master of the situation than ever and easily the finest player afield'. The concluding League fixture of the same season brought Kilmarnock to Ayr for a match in which Ayr United required at least a draw to avoid relegation. Tolland's seventy-sixth minute header provided the only goal of the evening and 'the crowd yelled themselves hoarse'.

The following season commenced with a drawn match at Falkirk and Danny Tolland's position was a seat in the stand. He had already been nursing a grievance relating to an unfulfilled testimonial match. He missed the first three League fixtures before becoming reacquainted with his black-and-white-hooped shirt. Then, in January 1932, he ceased to be selected. During 1931/32 Everton opened negotiations for him but there was an unexpected hitch when matters were close to completion. For 1932/33 he was farmed out to Galston who played in the Scottish Alliance. In effect Galston comprised an Ayr United reserve team and he was only recalled fleetingly. It was a situation which brought a scathing rebuke in the *Ayr Advertiser* in the aftermath of a 4-1 defeat against Queen's Park at Hampden on Christmas Eve. 'Why is Danny Tolland not included in the Ayr team? On Saturday he was seen carrying the lemons at half-time. Or were they oranges?' In March 1933 he was granted a free transfer, having made it plain that he was unhappy at having to play for Galston. Interest was high but his would-be suitors cooled on hearing his personal terms. That summer he joined Northampton Town.

Despite being in the Third Division (South), Northampton, including Danny Tolland, won 2-0 at Huddersfield in a fourth-round FA Cup tie on 27 January 1934. To put it into context, Huddersfield Town finished that season as runners-up in the Football League, just three points behind Arsenal. A further transfer took him to Bristol Rovers in December 1937. Immediately it was reported that the irate Northampton public had arranged a protest meeting to demand that the club should get him back. It was to no avail. The career of Danny Tolland ended with the outbreak of war and he eventually settled in America.

	League		Ayr Charity Cup		Scottish Cup	
	Apps	Goals	Apps	Goals	Apps	Goals
1924/25	13	2	1	0	2	2
1925/26	29	9	0	0	1	0
1926/27	31	12	1	1	1	1
1927/28	32	9	1	0	2	0
1928/29	25	4	–	–	3	2
1929/30	37	5	2	0	2	2
1930/31	31	6	–	–	3	3
1931/32	23	3	0	0	2	0
1932/33	5	0	–	–	0	0
	226	50	5	1	16	10

John Traynor was with Celtic until joining Clydebank in 1989. His next move brought him to Ayr United to make his debut in a 0-0 draw at Raith Rovers on 9 November 1991.

In his time at Ayr he would play either at full-back or in midfield. While playing in the latter position, he scored the only senior hat-trick of his career, on 1 February 1992 when his former club Clydebank lost 3-1 at Ayr in a First Division fixture. However, his main strengths were solid tackling and incisive passing. Another quality was an even temper.

The club's cosy First Division existence was put under threat in 1994/95. It was a season which lurched from bad to worse to diabolical, culminating in relegation. It was also a season in which John Traynor's appearances did not break into double figures. After playing against Raith Rovers at Kirkcaldy on 1 October 1994, his next appearance was as a substitute against Airdrie on 18 March 1995 and he was to miss yet more matches during the run-in. It would be veering towards fiction to suggest that, had he not been a long-term injury victim, he could have single-handedly saved Ayr from relegation. More realistically it can be stated that his influence was badly missed and that fewer matches would have been lost with a fit John Traynor on the field. Yet it had started so promisingly. The opening League match had brought Hamilton Accies to Ayr and, in a 1-1 draw, Traynor had equalised with four minutes left.

On winning the Second Division title in 1997, Traynor was key to the concluding 2-0 win at Berwick. He was one of the three Ayr players to hit the woodwork before the opening goal and set up Alain Horace to score the second.

The three seasons from 1996/97 until 1998/99 brought cup success over Kilmarnock with wins of 1-0, 2-0 and 3-0. These results came over a period when there was a huge turnover of players at the club, and it says a great deal for John Traynor that he was the only player to take part in all three matches. His Ayr United career would have been even longer had it not been for an incident on 10 August 1999. Raith Rovers visited for a Bell's League Challenge Cup tie which was low key. He sustained a dislocated elbow. The reality was that he played no more first-team football and was released at the end of the season.

His comeback was his own testimonial match, a 2-1 defeat against Newcastle, by which time he was with Auchinleck Talbot.

	League		Scottish Cup		League Cup	
	Apps	Goals	Apps	Goals	Apps	Goals
1991/92	25	4	2	0	–	–
1992/93	36	7	2	0	1	0
1993/94	34 +8	3	1	0	1	0
1994/95	8 +2	2	0	0	1	0
1995/96	20 +4	0	1	0	0	0
1996/97	30 +5	2	1	0	1 +2	0
1997/98	29 +6	2	3	0	0	0
1998/99	22 +10	0	3	0	1 +3	0
1999/00	1	0	0	0	0	0
	205	20	13	0	5	0
	+35 sub. listings				+5 sub. listings	

When Andy Walker arrived at Ayr United aged thirty-three, he had a first-class CV. His career had taken him from Baillieston Juniors to Motherwell to Celtic to Newcastle United (on loan) to Bolton Wanderers to Celtic again and then Sheffield United. Although acquired from Sheffield United, he had played for Hibs and Raith Rovers during 1997/98. He won 3 Scotland caps.

Initially, Walker agreed a one-month deal at Ayr. Ian Ferguson was struggling with injury, so the Walker arrangement appeared eminently sensible. In recognition of his form, the deal was extended.

After signing on 3 August 1998, he went straight into the team a day later. That match, a Tuesday evening fixture at Falkirk, was lost 1-0, although consistency in the matter of away form was forthcoming. Between September and November, six consecutive away League fixtures were won; one short of the club record set up in 1958/59. Walker was involved in the thick of that action. 'Robertson cut the ball back to Andy Walker who had his back to goal but he turned and scored with a vicious shot, high into the net' – Hamilton Accies 1 Ayr United 3, 31 October 1998. That was a typically opportunistic goal.

He developed an understanding with Glynn Hurst. By the end of the season it was possible to look back on a campaign in which the partnership had yielded 39 competitive goals. In fact one more Walker goal would have put them on 20 each. Yet the mention of Andy Walker tends to induce conversation about just one goal. On 23 January 1999, he stepped up to take a penalty kick against Kilmarnock. Nine minutes remained and he succeeded in putting the ball past Gordon Marshall to make it 2-0. This was not the goal he remains remembered for. That came two

minutes later! Once more he stepped up at the Somerset Road end to beat Gordon Marshall from the penalty spot. This goal is part of local football legend because of the manner in which the ball was struck. Perhaps the word 'struck' is inappropriate. He gently chipped the ball into the centre of the goal.

At this stage of his career, the passage of time had been kind to Andy Walker. His speed, fitness and general appearance all combined to give an illusion that he was much younger than he really was. Then, in the summer of 1999, it began to emerge that his days at the club were possibly over. He failed to agree terms on a new contract. In a newspaper article he criticised Ayr United for lack of ambition. It was difficult to reconcile this opinion with his next move, to Carlisle United, who had escaped relegation from the Football League in the final match of 1998/99. It was an escape created by a stoppage-time goal from a goalkeeper who had ventured upfield in desperation. In September 1999, Walker went to Partick Thistle, reportedly on loan, although he did not return to Carlisle United. After a brief spell with Partick Thistle, he was unattached prior to joining Kilwinning Rangers in November 1999. During the following month, he went to Alloa Athletic, having not kicked a ball for Kilwinning, each game having been postponed during his time there. He soon found himself assisting in eliminating Kilmarnock from the third round of the Scottish Cup in consecutive years. After a 0-0 draw at Rugby Park, he set up the only goal in the Recreation Park replay.

After hanging up his boots, he became a pundit on radio and television and made one more appearance at Somerset Park. That was in March 2001 when he played in a warm-up match prior to John Traynor's testimonial.

It is beyond doubt that Walker scored the cheekiest penalty kick ever at Somerset Park. Yet it would be remiss to lose sight of his other good work in the Ayr United cause.

	League		Scottish Cup		League Cup	
	Apps	Goals	Apps	Goals	Apps	Goals
1998/99	31	15	4	3	3	1
	+3 sub. listings					

At the age of seventeen, Davy Wells joined Ayr United from Auchinleck Talbot during the 1970 close season. By September that year, Dick Malone was unsettled at the club. At that point Ally MacLeod unhesitatingly stated that 'Davy Wells was going to be a great full-back in the Malone mould'. Malone's transfer to Sunderland took place in the following month but Davy Wells was allowed to continue maturing in the reserves. His first team debut came on 17 April 1971, at home to Cowdenbeath. In the second minute of the match, Wells sent in a free-kick which Alex Ingram headed to Phil McGovern who scored. Cowdenbeath ultimately won 2-1. In a pre-match comment Ally MacLeod had stated: 'We'll either win 7-0 or Cowdenbeath will collect their first win at Somerset Park in living memory.'

In season 1971/72 he did not appear in the first team until the occasion of a third-round Scottish Cup tie against Clyde at Shawfield. He was retained for a return visit to Shawfield for a League engagement a week later but Ally MacLeod then reverted to selecting the more experienced Jim McFadzean. By the end of the season Ayr United were the Reserve League champions of Scotland so at least it was a positive experience for young Wells.

On 25 November 1972, his performance in a 2-1 win at home to Dundee was immaculate. From that date onwards he became a first-team regular. Ayr United's season then went from strength to strength and this was reflected in the form of Davy Wells. His main attributes were being strong in the tackle and fast on the overlap. On 13 February 1972, he sat out a Scotland v. England Under-23 international as a substitute. Yet at least he had been recognised.

Wells was especially brilliant in the club's Scottish Cup run in 1973. In the first minute of the Hampden semi-final, he took the free-kick which Alex Ingram headed into the Rangers net. It was controversially disallowed for offside. In the quarter-finals he had been involved in three of the five goals against Partick Thistle. Transfer speculation was constant.

The career of Davy Wells was occasionally punctuated by spells of injury. For example, in

1974/75, he suffered torn ligaments. A further hindrance was a broken jaw sustained during a visit from Aberdeen on 10 April 1976. On being relegated from the Premier Division in 1978, experienced players were released but Wells was retained for the forthcoming challenge in the First Division. In fact he was the club captain when Ayr United entered season 1978/79. There was a memorable match for Davy Wells at Somerset Park on the evening of 7 March 1979. With both Ayrshire clubs in contention for promotion, this derby match was poised at 1-1 until three minutes from the end. Brian McLaughlin then swung over a corner and Wells darted into the penalty area to score the winner with a header. In the previous month he had scored with a header against Stirling Albion but the impact of hitting the target against Kilmarnock was somewhat different!

On entering his tenth season at the club he still possessed the stamina to race upfield just as effectively as he had done in his teens. Alas, the opportunity to do so was on the brink of being denied. Billy McColl became the favoured right-back. Wells was released at the end of season 1979/80 and he moved to Glenafton Athletic.

UNDER 23 INTERNATIONAL — SCOTLAND v ENGLAND

SCOTLAND POOL

ALAN ROUGH
Partick Thistle
TOM McALLISTER
Sheffield United
STEWART KENNEDY
Falkirk
DAVIE WELLS
Ayr United
DANNY McGRAIN
Celtic
WILLIE YOUNG
Aberdeen
PAT McCLUSKEY
Celtic
ASA HARTFORD
West Bromwich Albion
JIMMY BONE
Norwich City
IAN PHILLIP
Crystal Palace
JOHN DOYLE
Ayr United
DEREK PARLANE
Rangers
ALEC CROPLEY
Hibs

Trainer:
HUGH ALLAN
(Kilmarnock)

ENGLAND POOL

ALAN STEVENSON
Burnley
PHIL PARKES
Queens Park Rangers
JOHN McDOWELL
West Ham United
MIKE PEJIC
Stoke City
TOMMY TAYLOR
West Ham United
KEVIN BEATTIE
Ipswich Town
LEN CANTELLO
West Bromwich Albion
DENIS MORTIMER
Coventry City
TONY CURRIE
Sheffield United
STEVE PERRYMAN
Tottenham Hotspur
STEWART BARRACLOUGH
Newcastle United
JOHN RICHARDS
Wolves
TREVOR WHYMARK
Ipswich Town
CHARLIE GEORGE
Arsenal

Alex Cropley

Willie Carr

Trevor Whymark

Tony Currie

Referee: Mr. H. Wilson, Belfast. Linesmen: Mr. S.E. Paterson, Belfast Mr. J. Lorimer, Belfast.

TONIGHT'S ENTERTAINMENT
The Johnnie Walker Pipe Band appear by kind permission of the Directors of John Walker & Sons Ltd.,
Scotch Wisky Distillers, Kilmarnock. Pipe-Major - Tom Stewart.
Programme of Music will be selected from the following:-

SWEET MAID OF GLENDARUEL
THE JOLLY BEGGARMAN
LOUDON'S WOODS & BRAES
STRUY LODGE
BUCKSTONE DELL

FINDLAY McKENZIE
ARCHIE McKINDLEY
THE SKYE GATHERING
THE BLACK WATCH POLKA
D.A. McKENZIE

HIGH ROAD TO LINTON
LIEUT. McGUIRE
McKENZIE WARREN
THE HILLS OF ALVA

Pictures by Courtesy of the Daily Record

Printed by Walker & Connell Ltd., Hastings Square, Darvel.

Asa Hartford

Phil Parkes

On 13 February 1973, two Ayr United players appeared in the Under-23 pool for a match against their English counterparts.

In March 1984, Derek Whiteford left Ayr United to become part of a new management team at Dumbarton. This left a vacancy for the post of assistant to manager George Caldwell. That post was filled by Davy Wells. In December 1990, Ally MacLeod vacated the managerial post. Wells was his assistant therefore he became caretaker manager pending the appointment of George Burley who brought in his own man (Dale Roberts) in the summer of 1991.

	League		Scottish Cup		League Cup	
	Apps	Goals	Apps	Goals	Apps	Goals
1970/71	1	0	0	0	0	0
1971/72	1	0	1	0	0	0
1972/73	22 +1	1	4	0	1	0
1973/74	19	0	0	0	6	1
1974/75	18 +1	0	0	0	6	1
1975/76	18 +6	2	2	0	6	0
1976/77	24 +1	0	3	0	1 +3	1
1977/78	12	0	1	0	0	0
1978/79	32 +6	2	2	0	5	0
1979/80	3 +5	0	0	0	1 +1	0
	150	5	13	0	26	3
	+20 sub. listings				+4 sub. listings	

Sprigger White
Goalkeeper, 1912-1917

The Ayr United career of Sprigger White is perplexing to understand. Succeeding generations of supporters were regaled by olden-day memories of this player. It is also the case that he holds the club record for consecutive shutouts and that more than seventy years after his last game for the club, a pub in England was named after him. The perplexing issue is that he played comparatively few first-team games.

In 1912/13 Ayr United did not run a team in a reserve League. Instead, the second eleven was labelled Ayr United Juniors and this team played in the Irvine and District League. It is therefore curious that Ayr United had a team competing in the Scottish Junior Cup. On 26 October 1912, Ayr United Juniors drew 2-2 with Mossblown Strollers in a Scottish Cup tie played at Beresford Park. The Mossblown goalkeeper, Robert White, known as 'Sprigger', found himself making a League debut for Ayr United a week later.

That debut was at home to Albion Rovers and he was not overworked as the match was won 3-0. On the following Saturday, Ayr United travelled to play Arthurlie, again in a Second Division fixture. The game was won 2-1 with the home goal coming from a penalty kick. The following was penned: 'The test on such a ground was expected to prove a stiff one for the United's young custodian but he only got two or three shots which gave him any anxiety and these he cleared in an approved style. With gloves on he might have saved the penalty.'

Sprigger's position was further consolidated by a one-month suspension for Lee Massey, the goalkeeper whom he had replaced. Massey was destined to play just one more first-team game and even that was because Sprigger had an absence due to a family bereavement.

On the last Saturday in November 1912, Ayr United went to Dunfermline. Sprigger had played four League games for the loss of one goal, a penalty kick. At this time Dunfermline were the holders of the Scottish Qualifying Cup and the completed 1912/13 table would show them as runners-up to Ayr United. It was potentially Sprigger's toughest test. The result was a 0-0 draw after which he was described as 'a hero'.

From 16 November 1912 to 1 January 1913, Ayr United played eight consecutive matches without conceding a goal. All of these matches were Second Division fixtures and the goalkeeper in each case was Sprigger White. He established a club record which remains unsurpassed. In his first ten games for the club he conceded just one goal.

From 1913/14 onwards, Ayr United were in the loftier sphere of First Division football and the 'Shutout King' became the victim of an axe-wielding exercise which was a perceived attempt at strengthening the squad. He was consigned to the reserves and did not re-emerge to first-team football until November 1914 when first-choice Jack Lyall was ill.

Reserve football and fleeting League appearances became the pattern. It culminated in Sprigger's final appearance at League level on 21 April 1917. On that day he played for Raith Rovers who had arrived without a goalkeeper.

In 1988 a descendant of Sprigger named a pub in his memory, called 'The Sprigger's Arms'. It was in Dudley, West Midlands.

	League Apps	Scottish Cup Apps	Ayr Charity Cup Apps
1912/13	21	1	2
1913/14	NO APPEARANCES IN ANY COMPETITION		
1914/15	4	—	1
1915/16	NO APPEARANCES IN ANY COMPETITION		
1916/17	6	—	—
	31	1	3

His actual name was Quintin Young but he was popularly known as 'Cutty'. He was well known to many Ayr United supporters before signing for the club. Almost certainly this was due to his being a native of the Ayrshire village of Drongan which, in terms of supporters and players, has been an Ayr United heartland through the decades.

On the evening of 20 May 1969, Ayr United staged a closed-doors trial match against Partick Thistle. The venue was Voluntary Park, the home of Whitletts Victoria. One of those on view was twenty-one-year-old Cutty Young, then of Kello Rovers. Within a fortnight he was signed.

He was first viewed as an Ayr United player on 2 August 1969 in a pre-season friendly against Bolton Wanderers and he fitted right in as if he had been playing for years at this level. 'Yet another great display by Quintin Young' – Ayr United 4 Queen of the South 1, 16 August 1969. This was his third competitive match and he had already established good form. Cutty did not need time to establish himself in the senior game.

After winning a League Cup section, newly promoted Ayr United had then to embark on the First Division programme which began with an opening-day visit from Hibs. In that fixture, Cutty easily had the best of it in opposition to Hibs' experienced left-back Joe Davis. Three minutes before the break, Cutty was the victim of a bad challenge from Joe McBride. The resultant retaliation merited a sending off according to referee Currie. By this time Ayr United had a 2-0 lead and Cutty had torn the visiting defence to shreds. It was

reported that: 'Before being sent off, Young was the demoraliser-in-chief'.

'During the game Young often had Gemmell in a fankle' – Ayr United 1 Celtic 2, Hampden Park, 13 October 1969. This refers to his play in a League Cup semi-final replay.

Cutty had a whole repertoire of skills with which to demoralise full-backs. On 18 October 1969, during a 0-0 draw with Hearts, visiting full-back Oliver constantly fouled him. With six minutes remaining, he fouled Cutty again. Cutty angrily pushed him. He was sent off, but Oliver remained on the field. At the end of the match, feelings were running so high that referee Dempsey left the field under police escort.

At the outset of 1970/71, a three-week suspension meant that he missed the League Cup sectional ties. His return coincided with the start of the League campaign but there was no erosion of his skills. In 1969/70 Cutty had scored for Ayr United in a home win over Rangers. In 1970/71 he scored twice in that fixture, one an own goal! That was on 21 November 1970 when Rangers were trailing at Ayr to an Ian Whitehead goal. With seventy-three minutes gone, Cutty diverted the ball into his own net. Five minutes later he scored at the other end and it ended 2-1.

On 24 February 1971, he played for the Scotland Under-23 team against their English counterparts at Hampden Park. Coventry City were represented that night. In July 1971 he was sold to that club. Cutty later went to Rangers in a deal which took Colin Stein the other way. His career wound down with East Fife then Whitletts Victoria.

Although only spending two seasons as an Ayr United player, the impact he created gave rise to an illusion that his length of service was much greater.

| | League | | Scottish Cup | | League Cup | |
	Apps	Goals	Apps	Goals	Apps	Goals
1969/70	33	5	1	0	10	2
1970/71	32 +1	4	1	0	0	0
	65	9	2	0	10	2
	+1 sub. listing					